D0810148

The Sports Franchise Game

The Sports Franchise Game

Cities in Pursuit of Sports Franchises,
Events, Stadiums, and Arenas

Kenneth L. Shropshire

With a Foreword by Mayor Sharon Pratt Kelly

University of Pennsylvania Press

Philadelphia

Library of Congress Cataloging-in-Publication Data
Shropshire, Kenneth L.
The sports franchise game: cities in pursuit of sports franchises, events, stadiums, and
arenas / Kenneth L. Shropshire ; with a foreword by Sharon Pratt Kelly.
    p.   cm.
    Includes bibliographical references and index.
    ISBN 0-8122-3121-X
    1. Sports franchises—United States.   2. Sports franchises—Economic aspects—United
States.   3. Sports franchises—Social aspects—United States.   4. Cities and towns—
United States—Social conditions.   I. Title.
GV581.S57   1995
338.4'3796—dc20   94-46405
                                                                                          CIP

In memory of my father,
CLAUDIUS N. SHROPSHIRE, JR.

Now you will not swell the route
Of lads that wore their honors out,
Runners whom renown outran
And the name died before the man.
>   —A. E. Housman, "A Shropshire Lad"

Contents

Tables

Foreword

The movement of teams in professional sports is often referred to as the "sports franchise game." To mayors of major cities across the country, the efforts to keep or obtain a professional sports franchise is no game. The District of Columbia at various times has been involved in two major sports-related struggles—to keep the Redskins playing within the District and to keep alert to the possibility of obtaining a baseball franchise to replace the twice-departed Senators.

What we are keenly aware of, and what Professor Shropshire addresses in this book, is that a professional sports franchise is no longer the financial panacea for what ails a city. We can no longer pay *any* price to call a professional sports franchise our own because an often extraordinarily high price is what the owners of America's sports franchises are demanding. If we do not pay the price they demand, they tell us they will move to the suburbs or to another city.

The unpopular decision not to give in to the tremendous demands of some owners of sports franchises is the type of difficult decision that I had to grapple with during my tenure as mayor of Washington, D.C. Our cities today are confronted with a myriad of problems and have only limited financial resources to allocate. Our priorities must be readjusted.

This concise book causes the reader to take a step back and to reconsider sport-related expenditures. It also raises the issue of the social obligation that some owners may find that they have for America's inner cities.

The mayors of American cities are confronted with a prisoner's dilemma of sorts. If no mayor succumbs to the demands of a franchise shopping for a new home then the teams will stay where they are. This, however, is unlikely to happen because if Mayor A is not willing to pay the price, Mayor B may think it is advantageous to open up the city's wallet. Then to protect his or her interest, Mayor A often ends up paying the demanded price.

I do love sports. The presence of a team within the city limits is important. My father is one of the lucky season ticket holders to the Washington Redskins. My husband has been involved in a number of sports-related business ventures. I have a strong belief that sports should continue to be an important feature of Washington, D.C., just as is our nation's government.

I certainly do not agree with all that is presented in this work. But probably the most important thrust of the book, which I wholeheartedly agree with, is the need to rethink our priorities when it comes to spending on sports. Public monies should be used for the maximum benefit of all, not just those who happen to be sports fans *and* can afford to attend the games. It is the duty of civic leaders to protect the interests of all of their citizens.

Mayor Sharon Pratt Kelly
Washington, D.C.

Acknowledgments

Several people, in various ways, helped in the writing of this book. A list that may inadvertently exclude some of the most important contributors includes Natalia Bragilevskaya, Mark Brantt, Peter Bynoe, Maneesh Chawla, Robert Digisi, Tamara English, Peter Faust, Gene Ferguson, James Gray, Marty Greenberg, Rae Hall-Goodman, Carl Hirsh, Diane Hovencamp, Valerie Jarret, Michael Jones, Mayor Sharon Pratt Kelly, Roslyn Levine, Karol Mason, Rich Nichols, Eric Orts, Andrew Sankin, Joe Sedlak, Ed Shils, Bill White, and Terrie Williams.

Special acknowledgment goes to the National Sports Law Institute of Marquette University Law School for providing me copies or summaries of nearly seventy stadium and arena leases.

Thanks also to the Wharton Real Estate Center for providing the initial research funding for this work. Thanks as well to my longtime mentor, William Gould, for encouraging me to write this book.

Thanks, once again, to my wife Diane for putting up with what must have seemed like my endless work on this manuscript, and to my mother Jane for asking at regular intervals when the next book would be done. It's done.

Finally, thanks to my daughter, Theresa Camille, who arrived while the manuscript was nearing completion and cooperated (sometimes) by sleeping while I worked. And to my son, Samuel Warren, who arrived after I completed reviewing the page proofs, thank you for your timing.

Introduction

There is no way I can out-yes and out-giveaway Mr. Governor Giveaway. . . . This isn't my money. This is the money of the people of the
District of Columbia.
—Washington, D.C., Mayor Sharon Pratt Kelly referring to Virginia Governor Douglas Wilder during negotiations with the Washington Redskins[1]

Chicago and Philadelphia are now the only two cities in the United States
that can boast about having a full complement of professional sports
franchises—football, baseball, basketball, and hockey—playing within
their city limits. Other major cities have lost one or more of *their* franchises to the suburbs or to other cities. Until fairly recently, the owner
of the team typically also owned the downtown stadium. For example,
in 1950 the Cleveland Indians was the only major league franchise that
played in a publicly owned facility.[2] A lot has changed since 1960 when
a trip to the ballpark meant a trip downtown.[3] Today the trip is usually
to a publicly financed facility in the suburbs. Today the trip is often too
expensive for many individuals and families, particularly those residents
of the inner city, to make at all.[4]

The reasons behind the "fleeing franchise" syndrome are simple. More
cities that are already equipped with stadiums and arenas crave sports
franchises than there are available franchises. As this is being written
there are plans in the works or construction underway for at least a dozen
new sports facilities. A sampling of future construction plans are shown
in Table 1.[5]

Professional sports leagues possess a legally protected monopoly power
that allows each league to limit the number of new franchises. Without
question, the leagues use this artificially created franchise scarcity to the
fullest financial advantage of the franchise owners already in the league.
Why would a franchise owner pay for a new sports facility with private

TABLE 1. Sports Facility Construction Planned or Underway.

City	Facility	Estimated cost (in millions)	Scheduled Opener
Atlanta	Stadium (Olympics converting to baseball)	$209	1996
Boston	Arena	160	1995
Buffalo	Arena	125	1995
Charlotte	Stadium	160	1995
Colorado	Stadium (baseball)	141	1995
Milwaukee	Stadium	140	1996
Montreal	Arena	150	1995
Ottawa	Arena	190	1995
Philadelphia	Arena	200	1996
Vancouver	Arena	120	1995

Source: *The 1994 Information Please Almanac*, ed. Mike Meserole (Boston: Houghton Mifflin Company, 1994), 492–493, as updated and edited by author. Unless specifically designated, "stadium" denotes either baseball or football and "arena" denotes basketball or hockey.

funds when cities are clamoring for the opportunity to pay with public funds? Civic leaders eagerly compete to have a sports franchise call their city home. Like the children's game of musical chairs, there are facilities left standing and unused once the limited franchises are all taken.

The methods by which a community may obtain a sports franchise are limited. Possible routes include league expansion, league-approved relocation, obtaining a franchise from a newly formed league, or "stealing" an established team from another community.

What value does a sports franchise bring to a city? Why is the competition for these franchises so vigorous? When should a city battle for a franchise? Should a city only concern itself with the bottom-line dollar value of a franchise? Should a city build a stadium or arena in the hopes of attracting a franchise? These are some of the significant questions this book attempts to answer, and a host of issues must be examined before reaching constructive answers. These answers will provide a framework for understanding the true impact of sports franchises on a community.

It has become a cliché to say that sport is more than just a game—it is now big business. The annual "gross national sports product" is fast approaching $100 billion.[6] In the 1980s, American cities spent an estimated total of $750 million to renovate and construct stadiums and arenas.[7]

At the beginning of this decade, ten cities vied for two Major League Baseball expansion franchises granted for $95 million apiece by the league in 1991. Eighteen separate potential ownership groups put up $100,000 per group for the right to enter into the competition.[8]

In the 1990s, even those who weren't sports fans became aware that the annual salary for the average baseball player had exceeded $1 million. Indeed, games provide great financial value to professional athletes. A major sports-related trial also confirmed as fact what many have long believed: owners of sports franchises make a good living too. For example, in 1990 then-Philadelphia Eagles owner Norman Braman drew a salary of $7.5 million.[9]

The widespread media coverage of increasing player salaries is often accompanied by outrage from those who ponder the question, Should anyone be paid so much for their participation in a mere game?

Initial dramatic increases in salaries closely paralleled an increase in the revenues that broadcasters paid the owners of sports franchises for the rights to present their games to the public. As the players saw these broadcasting revenues increase, they made it clear—individually, through their agents, or oftentimes via their unions—that they wanted larger slices of the revenue pie, not unlike the shareholders, partners, employees, or participants in any sort of business venture.

Although the acceptance of sport as business is, in theory, universal, in general many people strongly feel that it is wrong for someone to receive such great wealth just for playing games. There is also a related view that star athletes with highly visible positions in sports have a duty to serve as role models.

During the 1992 riots in Los Angeles, there was considerable public discussion of the role athletes should play when violence erupts in American cities.[10] Some commentators criticized the small role that the athletes did play. Indeed, what were they to do? Help to stop the violence? Use their station in life to establish themselves as role models? Calm the citizens in the communities that were confronted with urban unrest? The argument is that along with their new-found wealth, athletes have increased social responsibilities. The message seems to be "Live up to your position as a role model and you will justify, or help to justify, the tremendous salary you receive." That view is based on memories of past celebrity role models, such as Joe Louis, Ted Williams, and other prominent athletes who donned their military uniforms during the wars occurring during their lifetimes.

Because athletes were noticeably absent from the ranks of those who tried to quell the violence in Los Angeles, *Sports Illustrated* asked T. Rodgers, a former gang leader, what he thought about this situation. Rodgers replied, "We are the role models in this community. [The athletes are] amateurs in the things that we're trying to do. This is my arena. I guess they could grab a broom, but there are two things we need— technical expertise and capital. Anything other than that . . ."[11]

We try as a society to impose on the big business form of sport many of the ethics and standards that we as children connected with sport. For the good of society, athletes who use illegal drugs have not been permitted to participate in sport because the wrong message would be sent to our children. Many people are astonished that substance abusers Steve Howe and Darryl Strawberry are being allowed to play Major League Baseball. In other businesses, individual employers decide whether to retain a reformed or reforming drug abuser. An employer that gives a punch press operator another chance most often receives high praise, so why not in baseball and other sports?

People sometimes fail to recognize that sport is not just a kid's game played by grownups. Often the same blue-collar worker who supported his union's strike for higher wages cannot believe that multimillion-dollar athletes exercise the same right. The teamster who would not have dreamed of crossing a picket line thought nothing of attending a replacement game or even participating as a replacement player during the 1987 National Football League strike. This scab played football as a boy and may consider that the game is not really work. He may have been one of the many who dreamt he was only a touchdown pass away from stardom himself.

Sport, in this broader sense of providing role models and guidelines for life, is arguably not only of value to the participants but also to society, and to cities in particular. These noneconomic arguments sometimes are most effective in convincing the citizens of a city that the presence of a sports franchise is important. In the pursuit of a franchise, it is often confusing to distinguish between the actual dollars-and-cents value of a franchise and other, less tangible societal values. This blend of the economic and social values, combined with the conviction that only a city with a franchise can be perceived as "big league," helps explain why cities ardently pursue sports franchises and major sporting events. The formation of sports councils or commissions in at least forty American cities, each essentially acting as a Chamber of Commerce for sport, indicates the significance of this pursuit.[12]

If our society believes that highly paid athletes must serve as role models, should there be a similar burden on the owners of these franchises? If this business is so singular that *employees* should readily accept a societal obligation, then shouldn't the *employers*, the team owners, accept the same obligation? Rarely has that obligation reached the level of popular discussion that the obligation of the individual athlete has. Occasionally, some discussion of this employer obligation is mentioned in stadium contract negotiations.[13]

This book will examine both the economic and social values of sport, as well as the value to a city of being considered "big league." Since several of these factors are subjective, I will leave it to readers to decide for themselves what is the true value of professional sports to American cities. This work focuses on the value of sports to both vibrant and decayed cities. Many of the discussions of the value of sports have developed from what, as Mayor Kelly wrote in the foreword, some term the "sports franchise game," the most common and well-publicized vehicle through which people justify spending public funds on sports for the good of a community. Chapter 1 discusses this game and presents a framework for the later chapters. Chapter 2 outlines economic impact studies, a key piece of evidence used by city leaders and franchise owners to convince citizens of the benefits of a sports franchise.

The next four chapters review specific battles for franchises within selected cities. Chapter 3 details the battle between Philadelphia and Camden, New Jersey, for two of Philadelphia's franchises. Chapter 4 begins the coverage of numerous moves that have occurred in the San Francisco Bay Area, including the arrival of the New York Giants in San Francisco and a legal dispute between the Seals hockey franchise and the National Hockey League. Chapter 5 covers the activities across the Bay with the Oakland (Los Angeles) Raiders.* The head-to-head battle between Baltimore and Indianapolis for the football Colts is described in Chapter 6, along with the decision to construct Oriole Park at Camden Yards to keep baseball in Baltimore. Chapter 7 reviews expansion of professional sports leagues generally, and the particular efforts of the Washington, D.C., area to obtain an expansion franchise in baseball. That chapter also touches on the efforts of Washington to retain the Redskins football franchise.

The final chapter summarizes the worth of a professional sports franchise or event, and considers when a city should continue to stay in the fray to obtain, or retain, a franchise or event.

The choice of which appropriate relocation competitions to examine was difficult for there have been many. A number of moves—those that are not the major focus of each chapter—are discussed throughout. The relocation struggles that were ultimately selected offer a composite of the issues the parties are confronted with in a typical relocation situation.

In *The Brethren*, authors Bob Woodward and Scott Armstrong detail the exchange of memos between the United States Supreme Court Justices concerning which former Major League Baseball players to mention in

---

*Portions of Chapter 5 are reprinted from K. L. Shropshire, "Opportunistic Sports Franchise Locations: Can Punitive Damages in Actions Based upon Contract Strike a Balance?" 22 *Loyola of Los Angeles Law Review* 569 (1989), with the permission of Loyola of Los Angeles Law Review. Copyright © 1989 Loyola of Los Angeles.

an introductory paragraph of a landmark decision.[14] The players actually selected were of no consequence to the ultimate outcome of the case; the selection revolved around the sports preferences of the individual Justices. My own sports preferences certainly influenced my selections for discussion here.

For better or worse, we will not be able to go back to the days of team-owned stadiums in the heart of the inner city. By the end of this book, the reader will gain a clearer or different perspective on the value of sports and a new insight into the decisions made by politicians and citizens to bring, or not to bring, sports franchises or major sporting events to their cities and to personally assess the true value of sports to American cities.

Chapter 1
The Sports Franchise Game

You can have Disney World and every major attraction, but if you don't have a team, in the eyes of the world you're not a big league city.
—Patrick Williams, president and general manager of the group that successfully obtained a National Basketball Association franchise for Orlando, Florida[1]

In *Bang the Drum Slowly*, a novel about baseball and life, the main characters are professional baseball players who pass time off the field with a card game they call Tegwar, "the exciting game without any rules."[2] The veteran players invite an unsuspecting "cluck" to join the game, and then they take his money in every hand, as the mercurial rules develop. The players find a fresh cluck to pluck in every new city they visit.

In the sports franchise game the veteran Tegwar players are the franchise owners and their clucks are the cities that want to host their teams.[3] Why do teams move? The obvious and most accepted reason is financial survival. But, as will be illustrated, financial survival is not the sole motivation. Sport is a unique business. Moving a sports franchise is not an easy thing to do, even when a franchise is in dire financial straits and good business acumen would dictate a move to a fresh venue. However, a move by a franchise can be delayed, or even prevented, by other players in the sports franchise game. If the owner is an Al Davis, Charlie Finley, or Bill Veeck he may have trouble gaining league approval for a move not for business reasons but merely because the commissioner or a fellow owner or two does not like him.

A sports franchise owner has limited options compared with the proprietors of other businesses. Like operators of fast-food franchises such as McDonald's, a sports franchise owner usually cannot just pack up and relocate when such a move makes good economic sense to the owner.

The guidelines for successful relocation of a sports franchise are not the same as those of a privately owned dry cleaning business, where the sole proprietor may choose to move to a site where customers may more fully appreciate the business. Sports franchises belong to a bigger entity, a professional sports league. The National Football League, National Basketball Association, Major League Baseball, and National Hockey League operate in much the same way as does a partnership.[4] The individual teams within a league share profits but usually not individual franchise financial losses.

Several key parties affect the sports franchise business, and to varying degrees, each party looks out for his or her own self-interest.[5] Apart from the owner and the league, the sports franchise business involves fellow owners, the athletes,[6] the competing cities, politicians, and the fans (who primarily are voting, tax-paying residents of the involved cities). More so in the past but sometimes even today, these fans forget they are taxpayers and do not always realize the consequences of urging their politicians to do "whatever it takes" to convince a team to stay, to attract a new team, or in some cases, to coax a team back home. More frequently, some sports fans and politicians now show signs of decreasing zeal. A major portion of the 1990 Oakland mayoral campaign that saw longtime mayor Lionel Wilson voted from office focused on whether the city should make the investment to bring the Raiders professional football franchise back "home" from Los Angeles.[7] Voters have refused to spend on sports in such diverse communities as Phoenix, San Francisco, Santa Clara, and San Jose.[8] But this trend is not absolute. The voters in Denver, for example, said yes to a tax increase to finance stadium construction. They wanted a Major League Baseball expansion franchise and thought that building a stadium was the only way to get one.[9] Partly as a result of that tax increase Denver now hosts the Colorado Rockies.

Although money constitutes the main reason cities fight over sports franchises, cities also admit that their civic image is almost as important a factor. Today, sports pages constantly mention incidents of cities trying to entice a team or of a team trying to move to a new area. Direct and indirect economic benefits such as increased tourism, arena or stadium rental income, sports franchise expenditures in the city, taxes, and employment are often mythically thought to be guaranteed by the acquisition of a professional sports franchise. Such is the proverbial carrot at the end of a stick that cities chase. In reality, the only reward a city that successfully attracts a sports franchise may receive is the public perception that their metropolis has been thrust into that class of cities nebulously described as "big-league."

The value of that big league label to a city defies accurate accounting. Some may perceive overhauling a city's image to be priceless. When the sports franchise game revs up in high gear, it certainly seems that virtual pricelessness is the value a team acquires. When the Los Angeles Rams deserted the inner city for suburban Anaheim, many civic leaders, headed by the late City Councilman Gilbert Lindsay, asserted that the situation must be remedied. Their position was that an expansion franchise was not enough. The "great" city of Los Angeles (and particularly the feisty councilman's downtown inner-city district) deserved a team with a "name"—certainly if Oakland and Anaheim had name franchises, Los Angeles should have one too. That was part of the hyperbole that eventually brought the Raiders to Los Angeles from Oakland.

Sports franchises and American cities are not alone in their pursuit of sports. Nagano, Japan, spent between $11 million and $14.3 million on public relations alone in its successful efforts to host the 1998 Winter Olympics. And planners estimate that the cost of constructing facilities for the Winter Olympics in Nagano will exceed $2 billion.[10] In an unsuccessful effort to land these same Olympics, the Utah state legislature approved expenditures of $56 million for the development of a site in Salt Lake City.[11] In its bid to host the 2000 Summer Olympics, the Berlin bid committee announced that tickets to all events would be free. This policy represented the forfeiture of $68 million in potential ticket revenue.[12]

The factor that seems to trigger most relocations today is the desire of an owner to make *more* money. The public reasons have ranged from complaints about the quality of the stadium or arena or having to share it with another tenant, to poor fan support or too small of a fan base. General complaints about the terms of the stadium or arena lease are often raised as the major point of contention as well. As the forthcoming chapters will outline, new revenue avenues for owners are limited. One key area of revenue that some owners began to tap in the 1970s is the luxury box, luxury suite, sky box, or executive suite. These seats, which are often elaborate suites, vary from facility to facility. Generally, such a suite is an enclosed area, approximately the same size as a living room, with a plexiglass front and great sight lines for the event. The suite may include elevator access, private bar, private restrooms, catering service, and customized decor. Generally, corporate entities purchase the suites at a price that includes enough tickets to fill the box with clients or potential clients or as an incentive or reward for employees.[13] The revenue from these boxes, which can be worth millions per year to an owner, are generally retained by the home team. Unlike other game ticket revenues, this income is not likely to be shared with fellow league members. From an owner's viewpoint, a stadium with luxury boxes is far more valuable than one without them.[14]

Currently, Robert F. Kennedy Stadium in Washington, D.C., is the only facility in the National Football League without luxury boxes. In 1992

Jack Kent Cooke, owner of the Washington Redskins, was in the midst of stadium negotiations with RFK Stadium while simultaneously proposing construction of a new Redskins Stadium in nearby Alexandria, Virginia.[15] The Virginia Senate Finance Committee conducted a study to determine its support for the proposed Alexandria stadium. The study found that the arrangement Cooke sought would take him from having the worst stadium lease in the NFL at RFK Stadium to the best lease in the NFL at the new Virginia site.[16] The Virginia plan would have required Cooke to pay one dollar per year in rent, with no taxes levied on the stadium, ticket sales, luxury box rentals, or parking fees.[17] The proposed Alexandria stadium would have had 331 luxury boxes.[18] The deal did not go through.

In the major sports leagues the revenues are divided among league members in varying percentages. Football teams split ticket sales, or gate receipts, with 60 percent going to the home team and 40 percent to the visiting team; baseball's split is approximately 80–90 percent to the home team and 10–20 percent to the visitors. Basketball and hockey permit the home team to keep all of the gate receipts.[19] Concessions and parking revenues are not shared. The home team does not necessarily retain these revenues either. Depending on the individual contracts, the stadium or arena owner or an outside contractor may keep the revenues, or there may be a split with the franchise-tenant.[20] Each arrangement hinges upon how well the respective parties fared in their stadium or arena lease negotiations.

National broadcast revenues are shared equally among the teams within the football, basketball, and baseball leagues. In football, for example, the NFL will receive approximately $4.4 billion or $39.2 million per franchise in total broadcast revenues from 1994 to 1997.[21] Of this amount, $1.56 billion is from the Fox Broadcasting Company.[22] The $39.2 million per franchise split compares with $32.5 million per franchise under the contracts that expired in 1994.[23]

In football, other than some preseason game exceptions, there are no local television contracts for the broadcast of games of individual teams. The NFL regulations do not allow individual franchises to impair the value of the national television contract. In all of the other leagues, however, the home team keeps all of those local broadcast revenues. A city with a large population, and hence, a large viewing audience, may be a more desirable location.

There is still controversy over just how "local" are revenues from "superstations," which invade the local markets of other teams.[24] A superstation, such as WTBS in Atlanta, broadcasts all its local team's games, in this case the baseball Braves, over national cable television systems. There has been litigation regarding how the revenues from the Chicago, Atlanta, and New York superstations should be divided among fellow league members or what type of fee a team or superstation should have to pay for such extraordinary rights.[25] Thus, overall it is clear that in all sports except for NFL football, the income a team can earn from television revenues varies depending upon the city in which a team plays.

A vivid example of the price a city may pay when competing for a franchise is instructive. St. Petersburg, Florida, has long publicly expressed the desire to be the home of a Major League Baseball franchise.[26] In 1988, St. Petersburg spent tax dollars to build a 43,000-seat baseball stadium, the Florida Suncoast Dome, purely on speculation. No team had committed to move to St. Petersburg, and no expansion franchise was guaranteed. Without a commitment in place, even *more* money had to be spent to attempt to attract a franchise. An initial prime candidate for the new stadium was the Chicago White Sox, who played in what was the oldest stadium in baseball, Comiskey Park. St. Petersburg officials, via Lear jet, flew in a group of White Sox executives to present a sales pitch on the city and facility. The city further promised White Sox owner Jerry Reinsdorf a $10-million loan if the team would move south. A city official highlighted the recruitment with the statement, "If there is something else the White Sox need, I hope they tell us."[27]

Motivations in the negotiation process are never fully revealed. The interest that the White Sox had in St. Petersburg may have been sincere.[28] Once the St. Petersburg offer was received, however, Reinsdorf headed back for further negotiations in Chicago. In Chicago he was not only aided by the St. Petersburg offer but by the statement of Illinois Governor James Thompson, who said, "I'll bleed and die before I let the Sox leave Chicago."[29] In 1991 the new Comiskey Park opened in Chicago. The old Comiskey Park is now a parking lot. The state financed $150 million in construction and also paid for the construction-dictated demolition of one hundred family homes.[30] The displaced residents were also paid $25,000 per household for their trouble.[31] The $150-million deal followed an initial $120-million offer that St. Petersburg knocked out of contention.[32] The funding for the new Comiskey Park came from a 2 percent tax on hotel and motel rooms in Chicago. The team will pay rent on the stadium only if the attendance at games exceeds 1.2 million fans per year.[33] The deal was approved by the Illinois State Legislature in a midnight session and passed by only one vote.[34]

Chicago is not alone in this brand of municipal largesse. In New Orleans, the Louisiana legislature granted to the NFL Saints all of the revenues from professional football at the Superdome except for a flat 5 percent rental fee. The state's $4\frac{1}{2}$ percent amusement tax was waived for Saints tickets. In a 1980s lease with the NFL Eagles, Philadelphia agreed to a ten-year rent deferment, to phase out a thirty-cent per ticket tax and to purchase a $1-million scoreboard and a Panavision videoboard.[35]

Cities have even agreed to give franchises outright monetary grants. The Pittsburgh Pirates received $15 million in 1985 from the city as an enticement to stay. The Montreal Expos received a total of $33 million from the City of Montreal and the Province of Quebec.[36]

These antics indicate that civic leaders perceive a value in professional sports franchises that call their city home. Another city "scared" into building a new stadium is Cleveland, Ohio. That stadium was built for the Indians baseball franchise even though the team has had a dismal attendance record. "There was a heightened fear the Indians would leave," according to one official involved in the transaction.[37]

Spending by cities that are courting franchises generally represent the largest sports expenditure a city can make. Other expenditures, such as bids for Olympic Games or lesser sporting events, can have a major impact as well.[38]

Do traditional economic measures of return-on-investment justify the expenditure on sports by municipalities? A review of studies of new stadium construction and franchise bidding warrants the conclusion that there is no clear-cut answer and that there are many issues to consider.

Chapter 2
Impact Studies and Other Quantitative Analyses: Inconclusive Conclusions

> If it is not seriously fought, a psychological depression could set in along with the economic depression which has hurt our efforts.
>
> —David Carr, former St. Petersburg City Planning Board member, on the fate of the city after it was denied a Major League Baseball expansion franchise following the speculative construction of the Florida Suncoast Dome[1]

It is politically expedient to commission an economic impact study in support of a position concerning the acquisition or retention of a franchise or the construction of a new stadium or arena. Presented in a strategic manner, the economic impact evidence can be quite persuasive. This chapter summarizes the conclusions and some of the analyses from a selection of these studies, in order to show the type of fuel— or sometimes water—that gets thrown on the flames of the sports franchise game. Sections of other studies are discussed in other chapters, but those mentioned here provide an overview of the general methodology and conclusions.

A major criticism of any predictive study is that the conclusions are necessarily based on assumptions of future conditions. These economic impact studies contain estimates of how much fans and others will spend at a given event, the projected attendance, and how long attendees will stay and continue to spend in the designated geographic region. These estimates include increases in employment rates and other positive economic activities that are catalyzed by the direct expenditure by these attendees.

The benefits measured are "direct" and "indirect." Direct benefits include revenue from stadium rent, concessions, parking, advertising, and luxury boxes. Indirect economic benefit is determined by estimating the indirect impact of those direct revenues on the geographic region.

Probably the most publicized predictions to date of great economic benefits, both direct and indirect, came from promoters who made a successful bid to bring the 1996 Summer Olympics to Atlanta, Georgia. In its proposal to host the Games, the Atlanta Organizing Committee claimed that the 1996 Olympiad would generate $3.48 billion in local economic activity.[2]

Criticism of this initial projection, which was developed at the University of Georgia, was quick to develop. One major miscalculation was that every hotel room was counted as being filled during the Olympics. The study neglected to take into account that Atlanta hotel rooms normally have a 50 percent occupancy rate.[3] Donald Ratajczak, the director of economic forecasting at Georgia State University, has estimated that the impact will only be $2 billion.[4] He surmised that spending by Olympics attendees would only be a cumulative $150–200 million, not the $500 million estimated by others.[5]

A widely cited impact study, relating to the value of franchises, was conducted by Professor Edward Shils of the Wharton School of the University of Pennsylvania. Shils's study of the impact of the Philadelphia sports franchises was published in 1985 and revised in 1988.[6] The conclusion of both studies was that the financial impact was a substantial plus for the metropolitan Philadelphia area.

The initial study received national recognition for its use of the multiplier technique and has served as a model for subsequent studies conducted for other municipalities by other researchers. Shils utilized what he and Wharton Professor of Finance and Economics F. Gerard Adams describe as a "conservative" multiplier to determine the economic impact of the Philadelphia professional sports franchises.[7] The multiplier is a figure that represents the number of times that a single dollar expended in a designated geographic area will be spent or "rolled over" yet again in that same region. This estimate assumes that subsequent recipients of the initial dollar are somewhat likely to spend it again in that same region. The more spending that occurs, the more employment and other economic measures improve, thus increasing the value of the indirect impact.

Several different types of multipliers may be used. The Bureau of Economic Analysis of the U.S. Department of Commerce periodically calculates and publishes Regional Impact Multipliers (RIMs). These numbers are available for specific Standard Metropolitan Statistical Areas (SMSAs). The Army Corps of Engineers also calculates multipliers for various regions, as do private consulting firms and academics.[8]

The multipliers are usually devised by statistical estimates based on annual state and regional employment changes. The actual method of calculating a multiplier will not be set forth here, but for the examination of the impact of franchises and events, the multipliers used to calculate indirect economic benefit have ranged widely from approximately 1.5 to 3.2.[9]

Shils concluded that in 1985 the impact of sports franchises to the greater Philadelphia area was $523,682,222.[10] Using a multiplier of 1.7 within the city and 2.6 for the overall metropolitan area, he concluded that in 1988 the impact had reached nearly $1 billion.[11] This was a 65.5 percent increase in economic impact over a five-year period.

Shils's 1985 study also made various recommendations to the concerned parties, including advising the City of Philadelphia to initiate a "sports committee" to formulate a long-range sports plan.[12] The city subsequently formed the Philadelphia Sports Congress. Now such committees are standard in both major and growing cities.

A work that staunchly disagrees with Shils and others was presented by Professor Robert A. Baade in a policy study funded by the Heartland Institute.[13] Baade concluded that the economic effect of constructing a facility, and thus "attracting" a franchise, was minimal and that municipalities should move cautiously in subsidizing the cost of constructing a stadium or arena in order to attract a sports franchise.[14] Addressing the dilemma that many cities confront, he concludes that the number of "leisure" dollars that individuals in a community spend on such entertainment-type activities is fixed.[15] Baade concludes that the arrival of a sports franchise in a community at best would cause a shift in leisure spending but probably would not create an increase in spending. Instead of spending twenty dollars at the theater or ballet, a consumer might use that twenty dollars to attend a ballgame—taking advantage of the new option, but not making a greater expenditure within the city. In six separate studies since the original one in 1987, Baade has concluded that key economic indicators do not change in any significant amount when a new sports facility is built or when a team relocates in that city.[16] The cities studied by Baade include San Diego, Tampa Bay, Seattle, New Orleans, and Denver.[17] Perhaps even more significantly, Baade has determined further that there is a "lower rate of economic growth in cities that adopt a sports-development strategy than [in cities with] development growth of other sorts."[18] Moreover, the jobs that arenas, stadiums, events, and franchises do attract tend to be of the low-wage variety and provide little impact on a municipality's tax base.[19] Ticket-takers, peanut vendors, program hawkers, and workers on short-term construction projects do not build up a very large pension.

Baade's analysis coincides with another economist's conclusion. Professor Roger Noll of Stanford University contends that professional sports franchises should not be counted on to attract out-of-town visitors.[20] He maintains that most fans who actually attend games come from the immediate metropolitan area. Furthermore, in terms of annual attendance figures for teams, the numbers that are projected represent 100,000 or so individuals for football, a smaller number for basketball and hockey, and about 250,000 individuals for baseball that continue to be recycled to reach the annual attendance figures in the millions for each metropolitan area.[21] Cities probably should not depend on sports teams to attract a large number of visitors to urban areas.[22] Noll maintains that the actual number of separate individuals annually attending games is 10 to 20 percent of the published annual attendance figure.[23] The remainder are repeat attendees.

As for the concept of constructing a stadium to promote economic development within a municipality, Pepperdine University economist Dean V. Baim examined the financial success of fourteen major stadiums constructed in the United States.[24] Baim discovered that only one of the facilities he studied was profitable. Especially noteworthy is that Dodger Stadium, the single profitable venue, was privately financed. Dodger Stadium had a positive net accumulated value of $5,854,110.[25] In calculating the profit-and-loss figures, Baim utilized this "net accumulated value" concept, in which the net accumulated value equals the difference between what was actually earned by a stadium and what would have been earned had the same money been placed in an alternative investment vehicle.[26] The broad conclusion from Baim is that publicly financed stadiums are not moneymakers for cities. Table 2 summarizes Baim's findings.

Probably the largest flaw in any of these analyses, a flaw that argues against stadium construction by municipalities, is the underlying assumption that the purpose of a city government is to invest taxpayer funds as a private money manager would. As Baim and others discuss, the function of a local government, as opposed to that of a money manager, is to pursue goals such as building civic pride, and encouraging indirect economic development. Generally, the duty of local government is to make decisions and take actions which serve the best interests of the citizens.

Baim also argues that if taxpayer dollars are spent to construct a stadium, and if the stadium is built within the city limits, it is most likely the taxpayer dollars of low-income residents that are used. Nonsuburban sports stadiums, therefore, are regressive and place a greater tax burden on lower-income individuals, who often cannot afford to purchase a ticket to an event, rather than on individuals with higher incomes.[27] Considering this reality, is it wise public policy to bring sports franchises

TABLE 2. Net Accumulated Value of Stadium Investments.

Facility	Years in Survey	Net Accumulated Value of Stadium Investment	Comments
Anaheim Stadium	19	($3,224,565)	Positive cash flow in 5 of last 8 years.
Atlanta Fulton County Stadium	20	($13,595,738)	Losses smaller in the 1980s.
Baltimore Memorial Stadium	32	($2,922,206)	1983 was the only year with a loss during the 1980s.
Buffalo War Memorial Stadium	21	($836,021)	No original construction costs; team left before 1973 season.
Cincinnati River-front Stadium	17	($3,666,056)	—
Denver Mile High Stadium	18	($1,033,661)	No original construction costs; positive cash flow in 7 of last 8 years.
Foxboro Sullivan Stadium	15	($1,742,555)	Includes tax abatement on private property.
Los Angeles Dodger Stadium	29	$5,854,110	Includes property taxes on private property.
Minneapolis Metrodome	3	($3,010,639)	Includes proceeds from the sale of Met Stadium.
New Orleans Superdome	12	($70,356,950)	—
Oakland Alameda Coliseum Complex	19	($4,887,798)	Positive cash flow in 9 of last 10 years.
Orchard Park	11	($19,479,606)	—
San Diego Jack Murphy Stadium	17	($9,372,527)	Positive cash flow in 1984; losses declined in 1981–83.
Washington, D.C., RFK Stadium	20	($11,032,655)	Includes $19.8-million payment by D.C. and federal government to pay off bonds. Positive cash flow in 4 of last 6 years.

Source: D. V. Baim, "Sports Stadiums as 'Wise Investments': An Evaluation," Heartland Policy Study, no. 32, Nov. 26, 1990, p. 6.

back into the inner city? This topic will be examined further in the final chapter.

Professor William J. Hunter of Marquette University, in "Economic Impact Studies: Inaccurate, Misleading, and Unnecessary,"[28] examines the validity of impact studies generally. He harshly questions whether impact studies should be given much credence at all or, as he puts it by quoting Mark Twain, "It's not what we *don't know* that hurts. It's what we *know* that just ain't true."[29] Hunter focuses intently on the multiplier and questions its accuracy. His conclusion is that the mathematics of using a multiplier will always make the most expensive project look better than the less expensive alternative. Hunter calls this the "Taj Mahal Syndrome."[30] According to his analysis, if a municipality debates whether to construct a new stadium or to repair the old one to attract a sports franchise, use of the multiplier will always indicate that new construction is the more appealing alternative.[31] Because construction is more expensive than renovation, more dollars will be multiplied to make construction the alternative with a more positive overall financial impact.[32] The key to Hunter's thinking is that there is a distinction to be made between economic impact and economic growth.

Naturally, any economic impact study should be only one of many elements considered by the potential decision makers. A study solicited by a party that is in an adversarial position should be viewed with extreme caution.[33] Those studies conducted by or for municipalities appear most likely to cater to the position most favorable to the respective city's action. For example, the Shils study was conducted in the midst of the threatened move by the Philadelphia Eagles to Phoenix or other possible venues, an influence noted in criticism by Professor Baade.[34]

A study conducted in Baltimore concerning the impact of the departure of the Baltimore Colts to Indianapolis concluded that the loss of the Colts only caused the city to lose revenues of $200,000 annually, a dramatically different estimate than those typically commissioned in support of bringing a franchise into a city.[35] Not surprisingly, there is a lack of information available on how cities have actually fared economically after franchise moves took place, which illustrates that most impact studies are crafted to support an advocacy role.[36]

There is one positive aspect that can be reliably attributed to some of the moves. In many instances, ticket revenues improve for the teams at least in the first year in their new location. The football Raiders set a team attendance record in 1984, their first year in Los Angeles.[37] The Colts football franchise set a team attendance record during their first year in Indianapolis.[38] Attendance also improved over the last year in their previous homes for the NBA Clippers and Kings.[39]

The projected economic impact numbers for events and franchises can be impressive. The 1989 Super Bowl, according to one study, brought $130 million to the Miami area. The construction of Joe Robbie Stadium, with private funds, had cost only $125 million.[40] The same study projected that baseball would bring the South Florida region $60 million per year.[41]

Owners exploit the figures from favorable impact studies to compel the host city to make concessions to retain a franchise, and to entice other cities to submit bids for relocation. Robert Lawrence, a Senior Fellow at the Brookings Institution, suggests caution to those who would rely too heavily on the impact numbers. "People like to think that there's a science to economic impact studies. But what it often comes down to is the imagination of the people who wrote the studies."[42]

Clearly, no matter what one thinks about the accuracy of these impact studies, one will likely conclude that the presence of a franchise is of some financial value to a city. Just as Hunter cited one Twain quote, another may be appropriate, with a slight modification. "There are three kinds of lies: lies, damned lies, and statistics."[43] Impact studies may be a combination of all three. Decision makers would be wise not to use impact studies alone, or even as a controlling factor, in issues regarding sports franchises, stadiums, or events. A study can certainly assist in providing some information for comparative analysis between potential projects, but the Taj Mahal syndrome must be taken into consideration. Broader noneconomic issues, such as the level of taxpayers' desire to dedicate limited municipal funds for sports-related projects, are questions that can be answered through voter referendums, taxpayer surveys, and other routes.

The next chapters describe the value that several representative American cities have assigned to sports franchises. These case studies illustrate some of the variations in the sports franchise game.

Chapter 3
The Philadelphia v. Camden Story

We've got to invest in the future of this city [and] this is not just an investment in the city, but in the Delaware Valley [the metropolitan Philadelphia region] and in the Commonwealth. This investment will pay dividends both in economic terms and . . . in hope.

—Pennsylvania Governor Robert Casey on the initial announcement of the construction of Spectrum II in Philadelphia[1]

We bring *Wrestlemania* in here, we have *Wrestlemania* going simultaneously in two buildings. That's 42,000 people in two buildings with giant video screens, each showing them what's going on in the other. And you could have one guy, in Spectrum I say, "I'm going to come over there and get you!" And you get the crowd in a frenzy in Spectrum II, and the next thing you know, there he is. He shows up in Spectrum II and he runs into the ring. Both places go nuts. You can just see it, can't you?

—Philadelphia arena executive Jay Snider on why the unique step of operating connected arenas is scheduled to take place in Philadelphia[2]

In many ways Philadelphia is representative of the fiscal disasters that may strike any major American city. The City of Brotherly Love has come close to financial ruin. Last-minute loans, bonds, and impassioned pleas to Wall Street have made Philadelphia the focus of much of the municipal planning world since the late 1980s. In the 1990s, the city has been confronted with a series of plans and deadlines. "Bailout" is the term that has been attached to many of these plans.[3]

Philadelphia is the nation's fifth largest city and has a team in each of the major sports leagues. At various times, three of those teams—the football Eagles, the basketball '76ers, and the hockey Flyers—have threatened to relocate to other regions.[4] Despite the city's financial troubles, all four Philadelphia teams continue to play within the city limits.

In 1991, the '76ers and Flyers threatened to leave. Curiously, the primary locale considered as a potential new home was Camden, New Jersey, a neighboring city—directly across the Delaware River from Philadelphia—even more financially blighted than Philadelphia.[5]

In recent years, Camden has been in the midst of an urban renewal program. Revitalization of the Camden waterfront included construction of the New Jersey Aquarium on the shore of the Delaware River across from Philadelphia. In addition to the aquarium, the plan called for the addition of a sports complex for both a basketball and a hockey team. Formulation of this plan coincided with the impending expiration of the lease of Philadelphia's basketball and hockey teams at the Philadelphia Spectrum.

The Spectrum was then a twenty-three-year-old facility—not in bad condition, but certainly not state of the art when compared with The Palace in the Detroit suburb of Auburn Hills or New York City's renovated Madison Square Garden. The chief shortcoming was the relatively small number of luxury boxes in the Spectrum. The luxury box problem, as indicated in Chapter 1, is often the factor that throws the sports franchise game into gear. Sixers owner Harold Katz and Flyers owner Ed Snider clearly wanted the additional revenue made possible by an adequate supply of luxury boxes. These team owners used their upcoming lease expirations as leverage to compel the city of Philadelphia to construct a new arena—one with luxury boxes and up-to-date facilities—to replace the Spectrum.

The new facility became the center of most of the public negotiations. Philadelphia Mayor W. Wilson Goode found himself in the awkward position of discussing the possibility of giving away city-owned property to successful businessmen Katz and Snider, in the midst of trying to lead the city out of financial ruin. This conundrum continues to be a complex one for financially troubled cities. Should they keep their teams at any cost? Essentially, was Mayor Goode willing to "bleed and die," as was Governor Thompson in Illinois?[6]

At one point, the competition between Philadelphia and Camden reached a level where the governors of both Pennsylvania and New Jersey, Robert Casey and Thomas Kean, stepped into the spotlight as the conflict neared resolution.[7] As the issue expanded into a contest between two states rather than just two cities, these state political leaders attempted to control the course of the negotiations.

Organized professional sports function today as a form of surrogate warfare between modern cities, a vestigial remnant of the actual warfare between ancient city-states that established the dominance of one region over others. In today's relatively peaceful political environment (despite continued hot spots in various regions of the world), sports rivalries and victories provide cities and regions with "bragging rights" that substitute for the actual political, social, and economic dominance of a wartime victor over subdued enemies (such as Japan and Germany after World War II). For example, there has long been political peace between the United States and Canada, yet it is a very significant social event when a Canadian team wins the World Series in baseball.

The Olympic Games are on many levels a model of international sportsmanship and cooperation, yet at the end of each day's competition the focus is on which countries won the most medals. The rivalry between the United States and the former Soviet Union that dominated the Olympics during the Cold War is an excellent example of sport as surrogate warfare.

Cities are not immune from this warfare mentality. The sports report during the nightly news informs us that "Pittsburgh beat Atlanta" and "Chicago was overpowered by San Francisco." When a sports franchise moves to another city (or threatens to), the reaction of city leaders is similar to that of a country whose army and navy are defecting to the enemy. The very act of raiding a franchise from another city—or successfully defending your home teams from "marauding bandits"—is another way our modern cities use sports franchises to play out warlike competition on an innocuous, socially acceptable level. The community leaders try to justify their actions as being in the economic best interests of the city or region, but their desire to win the battle against the competing city is just as much part of their motivation.

Would Philadelphia's teams have moved to Camden? Would the White Sox have moved to St. Petersburg? The "bluff" is a difficult one to call, particularly for a politician. Elected officials do not want to lose a franchise during their watch.

In the end, after a few more false beginnings, which included the decision to substitute arabic numerals for roman numerals in the name of the new arena and finally naming the two facilities the CoreStates Complex, the two teams renewed their leases in Philadelphia. And the deal cost the city. The plan negotiated by the parties mandates a new $200-million sports arena to be built adjacent to the original Spectrum on land provided by the city at the site of the old JFK Stadium, which had previously been condemned and was already slated for demolition. The state paid for the demolition of JFK Stadium. The original Spectrum will stay in place for various uses to be determined, with the one noted in the epigraph a genuine possibility, as are political conventions and sports championships.

For Philadelphia, there was at least a perceived positive result of economic benefit beyond just retaining the teams. Emma C. Chappell, the chief executive officer of the United Bank of Philadelphia, the city's only black-owned bank, voiced a general belief that building a new stadium "will lead to jobs and contracts for the people of Philadelphia."[8]

The Philadelphia franchise retention plan calls for the city, on the brink of default when negotiations began, to provide Spectacor—Snider's entity, which owns the Flyers and which will construct the new facility—with a low-interest loan of $6.5 million. This outcome was actually a victory for Philadelphia, which originally was to make an apparent grant of the $6.5 million. The final positive aspect of the plan was the long-term commitment of both franchises to Philadelphia. The 21,000-seat facility with a 1,000-car parking garage is scheduled to open in 1994, with the two franchises entering into leases that run for twenty-nine years.[9] The facility will include one hundred luxury boxes, compared with only fourteen in the old Spectrum. Each of these will lease for an estimated $125,000–135,000 per year. There will also be twenty-six balcony suites leased at $75,000 per year and superboxes at $12,500 per seat per year.[10]

Philadelphia's city government is not taking on the full financial burden. The State of Pennsylvania has committed approximately $12 million to construct parking, to demolish the adjacent JFK Stadium to clear the way for construction of the new arena, and to assist in other infrastructure requirements.[11]

One early sacrifice by the city in the negotiations was to allow Spectacor to retain future parking revenues from events at the new arena. These revenues are estimated to be about $2 million per year.[12] An additional issue discussed during the negotiation, one which received little press coverage, was a proposed condition that would require Spectacor to fund some of the public recreation facilities within the city.[13] This requirement could have made the municipality's financial contribution more palatable to many, since apart from the nebulous "economic impact," Spectacor's financial support of public recreation could have provided tangible long-term benefits to the troubled city. For example, approximately $2 million in annual parking revenues could have been directed annually toward youth sports programs. This arrangement could have revolutionized the relationship between professional sports franchises and the American cities that provide them with their markets and economic support. Philadelphia City Council member John Street stated that the funding of youth sports was not the duty of Spectacor or the Sixers, but was the responsibility of the City Council and the Mayor. The funding of youth sports was not incorporated in the final deal.[14]

The final selling point for the deal—and the factor that Philadelphia City Council members can cite as the reason they needed only sixteen minutes to pass the seven related bills—was the prediction for tax revenues once the new stadium opens: an increase of $2.8 million per year ($8.8 million each year, compared with the current $6 million in tax revenue).[15] According to the Commerce Department, the total gain in taxes over the sixty-six-year projected life span of the facility is about $2.7 billion.[16] One could argue that the city could have easily committed $2 million dollars per year from these projected funds to support city youth recreational programs; but this, too, was not done.

The outcome of the threatened flight of the two sports franchises occurred when Philadelphia was at an extremely low financial and spiritual ebb. Certainly, the fiscal judgment of the city could be questioned—even with the positive economic impact promised by the Shils study and other projections.[17] But what is difficult to measure is the potential impact on the spirit of the city of Philadelphia. The loss of a single franchise, as occurred in Baltimore and Oakland, can be quite depressing.[18] Philadelphia was confronted with the potential loss of two teams simultaneously. This certainly was a calculated factor in the tandem Katz-Snider threat.[19] The two franchises stayed even though the short-term financial benefits of Camden's offer far exceeded the final Philadelphia deal.[20]

Meanwhile, what was going on on the other side of the Delaware River? How did these developments affect Camden? One Camden official said:

It probably would have been sexy to have the sports teams here on the Camden side of the river. But when you look at the number of permanent jobs that would have been created, it's better investing the money in other opportunities on the waterfront. I never could see what the advantage was of having the teams over here.[21]

It is harsh to label Camden, New Jersey, a loser. A more appropriate moniker may be pawn. Would the Sixers and Flyers actually have packed their basketballs and hockey sticks and moved to Camden?

One reason why this move was more probable than, say, the White Sox move to St. Petersburg, Florida, was geographical. Camden literally is a good stone's throw from Philadelphia; the two cities are connected by a series of bridges and even a new ferry service. Many of the fans of Philadelphia sports franchises actually reside in southern New Jersey and in or near the city of Camden. Team fans who live in Pennsylvania could cross the bridges to New Jersey just as easily as New Jersey fans now cross the bridges to attend sporting events in Philadelphia. Therefore, a marketing campaign after the teams moved to Camden would certainly not have had to be as extensive as one for a team that moves from across the country to build a market from scratch.[22] Also, similar short-distance moves—traditionally to suburban areas, not to an adjacent blighted city—have been made in other sports. Notable examples are moves by the New York Jets and Giants to the New Jersey Meadowlands, the Detroit Pistons to the Palace in Auburn Hills, and the Los Angeles Rams to Anaheim Stadium in Anaheim, California. But this begs the question of whether Camden would be better off with the franchises than without, and the general issue of whether a city in such a blighted condition should consider building a major sports facility to attract a franchise. Economics aside, the big league city image is a key issue. Without its football team, the Packers, when would Green Bay, Wisconsin, be mentioned in the same sentence with New York, Los Angeles, and Chicago? Has the status of Charlotte and Phoenix risen by virtue of their gaining professional sports franchises? Clearly, it may be better to have a franchise than not, but at what price? There have already been economic studies that attempt to determine the dollars-and-cents value of franchises.[23]

Baade's study "Is There an Economic Rationale for Subsidizing Sports Stadiums?"[24] provides evidence that the financial benefit of municipal investment in major sports facilities is not always clear-cut. The available amount of leisure dollars may well be fixed, or at least severely limited. In a vibrant city with theater, movie houses, operas, symphonies, restaurants, music clubs, dance clubs, and a variety of other leisure activities, the spending patterns of fans of any activity may simply shift as new options arrive. Arguably, residents of a city like Camden have fewer leisure options. In addition, Noll's argument that few out-of-towners travel to sporting events may not apply so much when the out-of-towners need only drive across a bridge or use readily available public transportation to spend money in a city they would not otherwise visit.

In 1988, at the National Mayors' Conference, Camden was named the "poorest city in the U.S."[25] Camden is a prime example of the decay that many see in America's cities and find shameful. Camden was once the home to a number of major corporations and a thriving port city, and it is still the largest city in southern New Jersey.[26]

The proposed move to Camden by the Philadelphia sports franchises came when the State of New Jersey realized that what little economic vitality was left in the city was slipping away. Only two corporations continued to maintain their headquarters in Camden: RCA and Campbell Soup Company. Something had to be done to uplift the economy and make the city more than a place where disadvantaged people live, where others have to drive through on their way to somewhere better, or where outsiders come to watch nude dancers, buy illegal drugs, or purchase cheaper liquor than could be had in the state-owned liquor stores in Pennsylvania.

One entity that focused on Camden was the New Jersey Sports and Exposition Authority, which also operates the Meadowlands Sports complex in northern New Jersey. The Authority already had witnessed how cooperative activism at the city and state levels could improve New Jersey's cities when the brokerage firm of Merrill Lynch was persuaded to move their Manhattan-based office of over 2,500 employees to Jersey City. In that instance, the city and state partners pulled together a loan and tax break package of $15 million to entice Merrill Lynch.[27]

Both RCA and Campbell Soup were considering relocation of their headquarters away from Camden. Plans for development along the waterfront of the Delaware River, including construction of a new tourist attraction, the New Jersey State Aquarium, began to gain momentum. The New Jersey Sports and Exposition Authority and Camden's mayor at that time, Randy Primas, decided to approach the disenchanted Philadelphia sports franchises.

The timing of the combined state-city effort in the renewal of Camden may have been ideal for a financially troubled city that sought an image-lifting expenditure.[28] It was not as though the monies to be spent in support of these franchises would have been diverted from some socially beneficial program, such as building low-income housing or providing shelter to the homeless, since they would be drawn from an existing sports development fund rather than discretionary spending. Although the same type of fund should ideally be available for socially responsible programs, such programs unfortunately do not have the same "marquee value." Therefore, if Camden would have had the support of the state for *this* venture—with no discretion as to where the funds might go in the alternative—Camden may, in fact, have genuinely been the losing player in this round of the game by not obtaining the franchises.

The tension between sports projects and social projects was also present in Philadelphia at the same time. On the day one *Philadelphia Inquirer* editorial cited Governor Casey's praise for the arena deal (as shown in the epigraph at the beginning of this chapter),[29] another editorial preceded it.[30] The arena editorial ended with a three-word response from the editorial staff to the Casey quote: "We believe it."[31] The editorial that appeared above it, entitled "Rec Center Blues," discussed the deterioration of the public recreational facilities in Philadelphia. Would $2 million per year, or any other amount, have helped to alleviate the deficiencies that exist? The following is excerpted from that editorial:

Clever city workers. Even without a filtration system they manage to keep the water clean at the pool in Strawberry Mansion. It's simple enough: They just empty the pool *each day* and refill it the next time anybody wants to swim.

Across town at the Hersch Recreation Center in North Philadelphia's Fairhill section, the pool is permanently drained and at the moment contains the back of an abandoned car. Inside the buildings youngsters may find fire exits "inoperative, blocked, barred or secured"—as they were last fall when City Controller auditors visited—along with roach infestation, seatless toilets, and a leaky roof.[32]

Chapter 4
Shifts in the Bay Area, Part 1: San Francisco

Thinner than a 19-cent hamburger.

—San Francisco columnist Herb Caen in 1992, describing the odds of the Giants staying in San Francisco[1]

Perhaps the most publicized and longest-running relocation saga took place in the San Francisco Bay Area. Curiously, setting aside the former Oakland Raiders for a moment, San Francisco was one of the three cities that were involved in the first "modern-day" relocations. These are referred to as the modern-day relocations because they were the first moves made not simply for financial survival but for greater financial success.

The relocation of franchises is not a new phenomenon. In the formative years of professional sports leagues, during the first half of this century, franchises moved frequently.[2] Although the moves then were made largely for financial reasons, they were not initiated for greater financial gain but for actual financial survival. In a few cases, franchises relocated in order to join a new league. Large cities such as Chicago, Boston, and Cleveland lost sports teams as did smaller communities such as Grand Rapids, Michigan, Kankakee, Illinois, Oshkosh, Wisconsin, Hammond, Indiana, and Waterloo, Iowa.[3]

The Baltimore Orioles were involved in what was probably the first major franchise relocation. In 1903, the original Baltimore Orioles, which belonged to the National League, moved to New York and became the New York Highlanders.[4] The Highlanders eventually became the Yankees. Very few major United States cities have avoided participation in the pursuit of sports franchises.

The first major move by a franchise to increase profits was in the late

1950s. The highly successful Brooklyn Dodgers moved west to Los Angeles in 1958, followed that same year by the New York Giants, who went to San Francisco. Indeed, the move by the Dodgers is probably the most infamous relocation of all time.

Although early movement of franchises between cities existed in the then-minor sports of football and basketball, baseball had appeared stable. From the 1903 move by the Orioles until 1952, major league baseball teams stayed put.[5] However, in 1952, this serenity was disrupted by the Boston Braves. Their move to Milwaukee was the true precursor to modern sports franchise movement.

The 1952 Boston Braves finished seventh in the National League, and not many in Boston rooted for them. The franchise drew only 281,278 fans during that year and unsuccessfully competed for fans with the American League Red Sox, Boston's other major league baseball team.[6] With the dominating presence of the Red Sox and no upswing in fan support in sight, the Braves realized that successful marketing of a sports team is determined by the key sales factor cited in the old real estate adage: "location, location, location." The Braves moved the team to Milwaukee, Wisconsin, in 1953, and there was almost an immediate turnaround in fan support and related financial success.[7] The 1953 Milwaukee Braves saw their attendance soar from 281,278 fans during their final year in Boston to 1.8 million fans during their first year in their new home, and they also performed better on the field. In 1953, the Braves finished in second place.[8]

The city of Milwaukee also benefitted, as the Braves reportedly churned an additional $25.3 million per year into the local economy.[9] Neither the city nor the franchise could foresee at that point, however, that this success would not go on forever. Little more than a dozen years later, in 1966, the Braves left their Milwaukee home for Atlanta, Georgia.

Milwaukee was one of the first cities in this new era to finance the construction of a new stadium to accommodate an incoming franchise. As a result, having lured the Braves and then lost them, Milwaukee and the Braves were the first city-team couple to enter an enchanted partnership that at first seemed to be right out of *Camelot*; but, just as in the popular musical of that time, the relationship was doomed once a new suitor arrived. Since then, it has become common for municipalities to finance stadiums to either lure or keep teams, and private ownership of stadiums has become the exception.

Other major league baseball teams witnessed this early success and decided to relocate. In 1954, the St. Louis Browns moved to Baltimore and became the new Orioles, and in 1955 the Philadelphia Athletics moved to Kansas City for a brief hiatus until their next move to Oakland in 1968. These two teams suffered from basically the same syndrome as did the Boston Braves; they were the "second string" team in a city, and they moved because the cities seemed only able to support one of the two franchises.[10] In these cases, though, the Athletics and the Browns/Orioles simply remained poor-performing teams in new locations.

This franchise movement was apparently observed carefully by Brooklyn Dodger owner Walter O'Malley. The Dodgers were in the unique position of playing in one of the few cities that could, and usually did, have sufficient fans to support *three* baseball franchises: the Dodgers, Giants, and Yankees. At the gate, the Dodgers and Yankees did exceptionally well. In earlier times the Giants had fared well also.[11] In 1957, however, the Giants' attendance was down to 600,000 for the year.[12] The Yankees had few complaints, but the Dodgers and Giants were not happy with their respective aging stadiums, Ebbets Field and the Polo Grounds.[13] This gripe would become commonplace among subsequent team owners.

Dodgers owner O'Malley was determined to rectify the aged stadium problem.[14] He was able to garner a unique level of support from his fellow team owners. The league granted permission to move to a new city if a new stadium was not built in Brooklyn. The permission was only complicated by the additional requirement that the Dodgers could move to Los Angeles only if the New York Giants moved to San Francisco.[15]

That proviso brought Giants owner Horace Stoneham's hand to the forefront. O'Malley masterfully orchestrated a meeting between Stoneham and San Francisco Mayor George Christopher. Around that same time, Christopher stated, "They'll [the Giants] add at least $25 million a year to our economy," thus positioning San Francisco in the franchise game.[16]

The league was not necessarily trying to give O'Malley any additional leverage. Its main concern was controlling the cost of team travel for all league members. With two teams on the West Coast, a West Coast "swing" by the primarily eastern-based teams would be more economical. Another concern was the continuation of the rivalry between the two teams that had been developed in New York. The crosstown rivalry would be transposed to a cross-state rivalry.

The O'Malley organization showed an awareness of the power a sports franchise can wield. In an interview, then-Dodger executive Buzzie Bavasi told *Business Week*, "We feel the Dodgers belong in Brooklyn. We want to stay there. Walter [O'Malley] will even put up $4 million, if the city will put up the $3 million more it takes [to build a new stadium]." When asked what the Dodgers would do if the city refused, Bavasi replied, "Then we move."[17] The final, telling response was to the query of "Where?" Bavasi broadcasted, "[S]omewhere. Anywhere. We'll have to. Could be Jersey City. Could be Montreal. Could be Los Angeles."[18] The

Dodgers left an opening for others to bid for their presence while keeping the pressure on both Brooklyn and Los Angeles. Finally, the Giants struck a deal with San Francisco, the Dodgers with Los Angeles, and in 1958, major league baseball arrived on the West Coast. Dodger Stadium was one of the few privately owned stadiums to be constructed during this post-1950s era. In addition, as the Baim study cited in Chapter 2 indicated, Dodger Stadium has been one of the few to operate profitably.[19] In response to those who questioned the impact of the Giants' move on the youth of New York, Stoneham said, "Tell the kids I haven't seen their fathers at the ballpark lately."[20]

Shortly after these moves were announced, the press predicted more moves resulting from the domino effect. The most widely circulated story had the Cincinnati Reds moving to New York to fill the void created by the departure of the two franchises.[21] Reds owner Powell Crossley, Jr. used the openings in New York in his campaign to have a new stadium constructed in Cincinnati, telling a Cincinnati newspaper that the team would leave "if we can do better elsewhere."[22]

Ironically, in recent years, the Giants have had a grievance with San Francisco similar to that of the Brooklyn Dodgers in 1958. The main problem is a cold, windy, and outdated stadium, Candlestick Park. The Giants, arguably, have made more than the traditional effort to stay in San Francisco. Three times they have been involved with presenting measures to Bay Area voters to build a new stadium to keep the team in town. Three times prior to a 1992 referendum, Bay Area voters refused.[23]

Bob Lurie, the owner of the Giants through 1992 and the leader in the efforts to keep the team in the San Francisco area, obtained majority interest in the team in 1976 at least in part to prevent it from moving to Toronto.[24] In 1992, Lurie's Giants tried for the fourth time to stay in the Bay Area. Lurie made it clear that if this fourth measure did not pass, he was not trying a fifth time.[25] Measure G was placed before the taxpayers of San Jose to provide the funds to build a stadium in the city, the third-largest city in California behind Los Angeles and San Diego and the eleventh largest in the country.[26] Apparently not fearing political rebuke for spending on sports, San Jose Mayor Susan Hammer was a leading supporter of the measure.[27] Measure G would have required the city to spend millions on a $265-million project to bring the team to San Jose.[28] On election day, Bob Lurie suffered his fourth strike—the measure failed, with only 45.5 percent of the voters showing approval: 94,466 to 78,809.[29] If the measure had passed, the stadium would have been financed by increasing utility fees, with the average household utility fee increasing 2 percent or $35 per year.[30] There was a public-private partnership element to this measure. Lurie agreed to pay $30 million toward the San Jose venture and to cover any construction cost overruns.[31]

Following the defeat, Lurie stated that he had no choice but to move the Giants to a new location. He did not quote the Dodger's Buzzie Bavasi, but he easily could have said, "Somewhere. Anywhere."[32] Even then baseball Commissioner Fay Vincent, in a surprising action for a commissioner who had spoken strongly against relocations, initially gave his public support for a move by Lurie.[33]

San Francisco Mayor Frank Jordan formed a "blue-ribbon sports task force," the not-so-unusual step in these situations, to study the problem.[34] San Francisco 49ers owner Eddie DeBartolo proposed that the Giants and 49ers discuss constructing a new stadium in the city jointly. Lurie rejected this idea.[35] Other last-minute scrambling included twenty-seven unions discussing the possibility of pulling $200 million from pension funds to keep the team and sports agent Leigh Steinbergh trying to pull together a group of investors to prevent the move.[36]

It did not take long for Lurie to announce his decision to sell the franchise and that the new owners would move the team to the Suncoast Dome in Florida's Tampa Bay–St. Petersburg area. The announcement was made just over one month after the Bay Area voters rejected Lurie's plan for a new stadium. A group of five investors was prepared to pay $111 million.[37]

The sale was met by two predictable reactions: euphoria in the often-scorned Tampa–St. Petersburg area, and San Francisco Mayor Frank Jordan's vow to find a way to keep the team. Jordan and others forecasted the loss of the Giants at a cost of $30 million per year in revenues for the city.[38]

A National League team cannot be relocated without the approval of both fellow National League owners and eight of the fourteen American League team owners.[39] The National League owners voted nine to four to block the move to Florida. It was also appropriately anticipated that St. Petersburg officials, citizens, and other interested parties would file lawsuits for breach of contract on the part of Bob Lurie, violation of the antitrust laws by Major League Baseball, or both.[40]

In the 1960s and 1970s, financing stadiums through general obligation bonds approved by taxpayers was standard practice. This was not true in the 1990s.[41] In case Mayor Jordan did not get the message from four taxpayer votes, when a rally was held in San Francisco to "save the team," only 1,500 people attended.[42]

In the end a group headed by supermarket magnate Peter Magowan stepped in and saved the day for San Francisco. The group purchased the Giants from Lurie, pledging to keep the team in San Francisco. They stayed and had their most successful season on the field in years.

The San Francisco Seals: Early Relocation Law

San Francisco is not a hockey hotbed.[43] Until the arrival of Wayne Gretzky in Los Angeles, hockey was viewed as largely an eastern and northern (i.e., Canadian) sport.[44] However, San Francisco has experienced hockey in the past. One former Bay Area franchise was the San Francisco Seals. The Seals suffered in San Francisco from the obvious marketing problems. The Bay Area is not full of kids who skate on frozen lakes and ponds each winter; because of the temperate climate, there are no frozen lakes and ponds. Without the development of a hockey culture, the Seals were not likely to flourish. The owners realized this and decided that moving the team to a city where the hockey culture existed and did not have to be cultivated would be the best alternative. Vancouver, British Columbia, expressed interest in the team.

To most people, a steely-minded business decision by a team owner to make a move like this, a move to enable greater financial rewards, makes perfect sense. The problem the Seals encountered was the National Hockey League rule against unilateral relocations. The relevant portions of the NHL constitution provided the following:

Section 4.1 (c): "Home Territory," with respect to any member, means: Each Member Club shall have exclusive territorial rights in the city in which it is located and within fifty miles of that city's corporate limits.

Section 4.2: Territorial Rights of League. The League shall have exclusive control of the playing of hockey games by member clubs in the home territory of each member, subject to the rights hereinafter granted to members. The members shall have the right to and agree to operate professional hockey clubs and play the League schedule in their respective cities or boroughs as indicated opposite their signatures hereto. No member shall transfer its club and franchise to a different city or borough. No additional cities or boroughs shall be added to the League circuit without the consent of three-fourths of all the members of the League. Any admission of new members with franchises to operate in any additional cities or boroughs shall be subject to the provisions of Section 4.3.

Section 4.3: Territorial Rights of Members. Each member shall have exclusive control of the playing of hockey games within its home territory including, but not being limited to, the playing in such home territory of hockey games by any teams owned or controlled by such member or by other members of the League.[45]

The league owners voted against the Seals' relocation. The owners probably believed that some team must serve as the explorer, the educator, the marketer, the sacrifice in the market that showed resistance to hockey culture. To have a truly national audience for hockey, Californians had to be developed into fans. If the Seals moved, then whatever major league impact or exposure was occurring in northern California would be lost. A general goal of a sports league is to create new fans by placing teams in various regions.[46] A major benefit of placing teams in many geographical regions is the increased amount that can be demanded from a television network because of the increased number of potential viewers. The increased number of viewers will enable broadcasters to charge potential advertisers more in ad fees.

To some extent this decision may seem counterintuitive—do not both the league and the individual team owner have the same goal of making as much money from each franchise as possible? If a team can have greater financial success in another city, would not the league then be better off as well? Apparently, the location of teams in various geographic locations overrides the importance of an individual team's greater financial success—the marketing of the whole league to a large market is what is most important.[47]

This attitude is easier to understand in conjunction with the previously discussed methods used by the leagues to share revenues.[48] There are limited sources of income for a professional sports franchise: network television and radio revenues, local television and radio revenues, ticket sales, concessions, parking, and merchandising.[49] All of these revenue sources, except for the network revenues, are highly dependent on the city or region that the individual team calls home. In contrast, the network revenues do not depend on any one owner's success, but on the success of the league as a whole, since these revenues are shared among the league members.

When the Seals were denied permission to move to Vancouver by the National Hockey League Board of Governors, the team filed an antitrust lawsuit against the NHL.[50] The Seals based its legal theory on the Sherman Act, asserting that denial of the right to relocate constituted a violation of section 1 of the Act, which considers it an illegal "restraint of trade" not to allow the owner of a business to move.[51] The Seals owners also alleged a violation of section 2 of the Act, arguing that this restraint by the NHL constituted an attempted monopolization of the sport of hockey.

Litigation on these issues in 1974 was virtually nonexistent. A *Harvard Law Review* article, "The Super Bowl and the Sherman Act: Professional Team Sports and the Antitrust Laws," briefly and theoretically examined the problem in 1967,[52] speculating that any league regulations "which restrict an owner's ability to shift his franchise—at least to a new territory—should be held illegal."[53] The argument was that the league restriction against relocations was illegal on its face and that any restraint on this severely violated the antitrust laws outright without the need for any further analysis. The *Harvard Law Review* article stated:

Territorial restraints are traditionally considered per se illegal [illegal on their face], for the division of markets necessarily has the effect of eliminating competition. There seems to be no reason why these restraints are particularly justified in the sports context, at least when a team is moving into virgin territory.[54]

This nascent view of the sports franchise relocation issue initially did not garner the support of the courts. The evolution of the law in this case as well as in the other Bay Area cases reveals the internal law by which a league and the teams must abide. This information is important in order to understand just what a team can legally do in terms of unilaterally relocating. Of course, from the viewpoint of a city, it makes no economic sense to pursue a team that legally cannot relocate. The decision by the court in *Seals* made any city's pursuit of a professional sports franchise a far more risky exercise.

In response to the Seals' argument that the exclusive allocation of territories violated the Sherman Act, the court held the line of cases in support of the Seals' proposition inapplicable to a sports league. The court said that the past cases

[a]ll deal with combinations of independent business enterprises competing economically with each other and with other businesses not included in the combination. . . . In the case before us the parties are not economic competitors, and the territorial restraints of which the plaintiff [the Seals] complains have no effect upon trade or commerce in this relevant market.[55]

The court essentially viewed the NHL, and apparently any league, as a "single entity." The logic was that for an antitrust violation to occur, there must be two actors—Macy's must act in an anticompetitive manner toward Gimbel's, but if Macy's makes an internal decision that negatively impacts their own shoe department, there is no violation of the law. When the parties are not economic competitors, as the court concluded was the case in *Seals*, then surely there cannot be an antitrust violation.[56] The teams are all in the same business, and they need each other for competition. Without competition from the other teams, there is no business. The argument contends that even though the teams operate separately, they actually work together as a single entity.

The Sherman Act section 2 violation argument by the Seals was that by not allowing the move, the NHL was conspiring to monopolize the sport of hockey—to keep any other league from forming. Presumably, the positioning and "imprisonment" of the Seals in San Francisco was part of the NHL's monopolization plan.

The theory may have been correct, but the court held that the Seals franchise was the wrong party to bring the action because it lacked standing to sue. Under the legal concept of standing, only the party actually injured by a particular act has the right, or *standing*, to go forward with the lawsuit. In the *Seals* scenario, the party injured by the action of the NHL in relation to monopolization must be a competing league, not a member of the league and hence an apparent coconspirator.

Antitrust law holds further in section 4 of the Clayton Act:

Any person who shall be injured in his business or property *by reason of* anything forbidden in the antitrust laws may sue therefore [emphasis added].[57]

The "by reason of" passage destroyed the Seals' standing. Past cases have held that in order to show that the antitrust injury was by reason of the forbidden act, the plaintiff must be within the "target area" of the defendant.[58] The target area in the case of a section 2 violation was a rival hockey league, so only a rival league, not the San Francisco Seals, had standing to bring the case.[59]

The law in 1974 required the Seals, and apparently all other professional sports franchises, not to relocate without league permission. So if a league was not amenable, the pursuit of a franchise appeared to be a waste of municipal funds. Indeed, the National Football League had seen no franchise movements since 1960. As the next chapter sets forth, the saga of the (then) Oakland Raiders football franchise would change all that.

Chapter 5
Shifts in the Bay Area, Part 2: Oakland

> You need some money to give to an owner to [get him to] move his club. Otherwise, they couldn't get an existing team. That's my opinion.
>
> —Los Angeles Raiders owner Al Davis in a 1987 interview, on how the city of Oakland might attract a football team[1]

Al Davis, the managing general partner of the Los Angeles Raiders, has long been referred to by many members of the media and by fans as a maverick owner. Some say his image is projected through the Raiders team, which has long accepted the castoffs of other teams, sports the color black, and has a logo featuring a rugged caricature with a skull and crossbones image and a patch over one eye. Davis's success, however, cannot be disputed. While in Oakland, the franchise had thirteen consecutive sellout seasons.

By the end of the 1970s, Davis had apparently decided that his team would have greater overall financial success in the Los Angeles market than it had been having in the Bay Area.[2] Although the Raiders won world championships and consistently sold out their home games at the Oakland-Alameda Coliseum, Davis saw greener pastures in the southern portion of the state. The Oakland Coliseum lease expired at the end of the 1979 season. If Davis initially had only vague dreams of moving to Los Angeles, those dreams became vivid in 1980. It was then that the Los Angeles Rams franchise moved from the Los Angeles Memorial Coliseum to Anaheim Stadium, approximately fifty miles south of Los Angeles.[3] It was this move that converted the Los Angeles Memorial Coliseum Commission (LAMCC) into a willing suitor. The Coliseum in Los Angeles, with a capacity of 92,000 fans, dwarfed the Oakland-Alameda

Coliseum's capacity of a little over 54,000 and was the "Grand Duchess" of sports facilities.[4] The Los Angeles Coliseum was able to offer Davis a luxury box package that would gross him $5 million per year once they were constructed, whereas Oakland's best offer only grossed $1.6 million per year.[5] Site of the 1932 Olympics and the initial home of the Los Angeles Dodgers following their move from Brooklyn, the Los Angeles Memorial Coliseum boasted a history that no other facility could claim.

The LAMCC was notorious for moving at the pace of the average ill-regarded political body.[6] When the Rams put the stadium game in motion, the commission simply could not offer satisfactory terms to retain the franchise. An undercurrent to the negotiations, particularly in the African-American community, was the perception that the Rams were not pleased with the direction the neighborhood had taken—it was predominantly black—or the complexion of the fans who began to fill the stadium seats—African-American and Latino.[7] Demographically, Anaheim in Orange County was 180 degrees removed from the South Central Los Angeles Coliseum. In 1980, at the time of the move by the Rams, the Los Angeles street conversations in sport focused on the shift from the growing black and Latino inner-city crowd in Los Angeles to the leisure-suit–clad, white, suburban Orange County crowd.

This flight-to-the-suburbs issue is, of course, not unique to Los Angeles. Often, there is simply no suitable site within a city's limits to build a new facility, and in those circumstances the flight may be justified. However, some cities have constructed, or plan to construct, new facilities on the site of existing inner-city ballparks. Comiskey Park in Chicago is a prime example. The new Comiskey was built next to the old one.[8] In a truly exceptional circumstance in Cleveland, the basketball Cavaliers are actually moving from suburban Richfield into downtown Cleveland.[9]

After failing to keep the Rams in Los Angeles, the LAMCC aggressively pursued other NFL franchises, including the Minnesota Vikings, who were in the midst of their own negotiations with Metropolitan Stadium in Bloomington.[10] At various times, the LAMCC also allegedly courted the (then) St. Louis Cardinals and the Philadelphia Eagles.

Both the LAMCC and Al Davis were obviously aware of the ruling in *Seals*. The additional barrier to relocating a team to the Coliseum was NFL rule 4.3,[11] a rule which read much like the NHL rule on franchise movement. The NFL rule at the time read in part as follows:

The League shall have exclusive control of the exhibition of football games by member clubs within the home territory of each member. No member club shall have the right to transfer its franchise or playing site to a different city, either within or outside its home territory, without prior approval by the affirmative vote of three-fourths of the existing member clubs of the League.[12]

This rule rendered the situation even more desperate for the LAMCC. Rule 4.3, coupled with *Seals*, made for a reluctant class of potential tenants. Rather than waiting patiently for the NFL to approve a relocation or to grant an expansion franchise, the LAMCC sued the NFL.[13] In *Los Angeles Memorial Coliseum Commission v. National Football League*,[14] the LAMCC alleged that rule 4.3 violated the federal antitrust laws.

In initial interpretations of the Sherman Act in the first half of this century, the courts determined that a blanket ban on "every" contract that restrained trade in any manner was inappropriate and not what Congress had intended when it passed the law. With this interpretation, the courts adopted a "rule of reason," which typically required the trier of fact to determine whether the agreement causes an unreasonable restraint on competition, based on the totality of the circumstances.[15]

The district court denied the initial injunction sought by the LAMCC because at the time of the action, the move by the Raiders or any other franchise was not yet near fruition.[16] Subsequently, when the Raiders' move to Los Angeles appeared probable, the LAMCC returned to court.[17] In that action, the district court granted the LAMCC an injunction that barred the NFL from asserting rule 4.3 to prevent the Raiders from moving to Los Angeles.[18] The Ninth Circuit Court reversed that lower court decision, holding that the LAMCC had not shown the probability of irreparable harm necessary to grant an injunction.[19]

Following protracted negotiations with the LAMCC and the denial of permission to move by the NFL, Davis decided that it would be advantageous to enter into an agreement with the commission to move the Oakland Raiders to Los Angeles.[20] On March 1, 1980, Davis signed a "Memorandum of Agreement" with LAMCC agreeing to terms for the Raiders' move to Los Angeles.[21] Nine days later, on March 10, 1980, the NFL owners voted twenty-two to zero, with five abstentions, to bar the Raiders' move to Los Angeles.[22]

Following the NFL's negative vote, the LAMCC renewed its action against the NFL and its member clubs, which included the Raiders.[23] In addition, the Raiders filed a cross-claim suit against the NFL. As a result, the Raiders were aligned by the court as a plaintiff in the action and placed on the LAMCC's side in the cross-claim lawsuit.[24]

The initial trial (the LAMCC against the NFL and its member clubs) resulted in a hung jury and a mistrial.[25] The second trial (the LAMCC, joined by the Raiders, against the NFL) resulted in a damage award of $11.55 million to the Raiders for the antitrust violation, trebled to $34.65 million according to the provisions of the antitrust law, plus $4.86 million in damages awarded to the LAMCC, which was trebled to $14.58 million.[26] The trial court determined, contrary to *Seals*, that the league was not a single entity and that by not allowing the Raiders to relocate, the league had committed an antitrust violation.[27] The judge issued an injunction that, after two years of delay, allowed the Raiders to move to Los Angeles.[28] The Raiders were also awarded another $11.55 million in actual contract damages for a breach by the NFL of the implied covenant of good faith and fair dealing.[29]

During the appeals process, the liability and damage issues were reviewed separately.[30] For clarity, the two tracks of litigation will be termed *Raiders I* and *Raiders II*. *Raiders I* focused on liability issues[31] and *Raiders II* addressed damages.[32]

In the initial liability portion of the appeal, the Ninth Circuit upheld the district court's decision that the NFL was not a single entity, and that application of the rule of reason in analyzing the antitrust issues was proper.[33] The court then confronted the question of whether the rule requiring league permission to relocate, as applied, was unreasonable. The Court of Appeals affirmed the trial court's decision that the league had applied rule 4.3 to the Raiders in an unreasonable manner.[34]

In regard to NFL rule 4.3, the court stated that the guidelines must set forth standards that are clear, including a "procedural mechanism" for review of a franchise relocation request.[35] The court suggested consideration of factors such as "population, economic projections, facilities, [and] regional balance."[36] The court noted further that "fan loyalty and location continuity" should be considered.[37] In addition, the court noted that the league should provide the team desiring relocation with procedures for presenting its case.[38]

In *Raiders II*, the final appeal in *Los Angeles Memorial Coliseum Commission v. National Football League*, the primary issue was whether the damage awards were appropriate.[39] Specifically, the court examined whether the trebled antitrust damage award of $34.65 million to the Raiders should be offset by the difference between the more valuable Los Angeles location and the abandoned Oakland location.[40] In addition, if offset was proper, the court had to decide whether the offset should occur before or after trebling of the damage award.[41] The court determined that offset was appropriate and should occur before trebling, thus reducing the size of the antitrust award.[42]

The other damage issue was whether the trial court's award of damages to the Raiders for the league's breach of the implied covenant of good faith and fair dealing in contract was appropriate.[43] The court concluded that such damages were inappropriate, since both parties had breached their duty to act in good faith.[44]

In effect, offset before trebling would have reduced or completely nullified the $11.55-million award that the Raiders won in the trial court. In testimony, Raiders owner Al Davis specifically stated that the net value of the Raiders franchise increased by $25 million simply by moving to

Los Angeles and surrendering the Oakland franchise.[45] If this was an accurate estimate, the Raiders may have been required to pay the NFL approximately $13.5 million rather than recover damages. If the offset came after trebling, however, the Raiders damage award would still have been approximately $9.5 million.

There was no final resolution of this issue in the Raiders litigation. This round of the Raiders saga ended with an out-of-court settlement. The offset concept was examined by one other court in a lawsuit by the NBA against the Los Angeles Clippers, in *National Basketball Association v. SDC Basketball Club, Inc.*[46] There, this offset issue arose again in the consideration of the damage award.

The Clippers basketball franchise had moved to Los Angeles from San Diego without obtaining permission from the NBA. The league sued, seeking damages equal to the difference between the value of the franchise opportunity taken (Los Angeles) and the franchise location surrendered (San Diego).[47] The court disagreed that this was the rule that the *Raiders* court handed down and viewed the issue there as one of antitrust damages and not as a basis for deciding the *Clippers* lawsuit.[48] Before the courts could decide whether this offset rule was applicable to the general relocation damage situation, the Clippers and the NBA settled, and the Clippers made a reported payment to the NBA of $5.6 million.[49] The offset model has since become a guideline for payments made by franchises desiring to relocate to their respective leagues. The payment made by the Phoenix Cardinals after their move from St. Louis is indicative.[50] The NFL owners permitted the Cardinals to move from St. Louis to Phoenix, on condition that the Cardinals pay a fee to the league that included an approximation of the difference in value between the St. Louis and Phoenix franchise locations.

Relocation and the Law of Eminent Domain

As the antitrust action by the LAMCC got underway, there was also a lawsuit filed by the city of Oakland. This action epitomized—at least until recently—the aggressive mind-set of cities that sought to retain franchises. A city has few options as to how to keep a franchise at home. If a lease is still in force, a city can bring an action for an injunction or at the very least pursue damages for a breach of contract. Milwaukee attempted this strategy to keep the Braves from moving to Atlanta. They were successful at the lower state court level, but the State's supreme court eventually disagreed.[51] Negotiating a settlement is the preferred route. The other method attempted is the exercise of eminent domain powers by the city.

Oakland initially pursued the normal route of negotiations with the Raiders. In reality, Oakland had a formidable opponent to overcome, the Hollywood glitz and glamour of Los Angeles with its large stadium and substantial potential revenues in ticket sales and pay-per-view television audiences. In contrast, Oakland is a blue-collar town with a small stadium and competition from a franchise just across a bridge.

When the city saw that their negotiating tactics had failed, it too went to court. Oakland's legal action was based on the law of eminent domain, which generally allows a governmental entity to condemn and take private property for some valid public use. This power, although inherent in the sovereign at either the state or federal levels, does have restrictions in the federal and state constitutions. A municipality's power to exercise eminent domain is generally outlined by state statutes. Such statutes also set forth the process that a state or city must follow to condemn property and incorporate requisite state and federal constitutional limitations, including the type of property that may be condemned, the type of notice and hearings required, and the measure of compensation that must be awarded to the owner of the condemned property.

These types of "takings" are typically of private homes or lots to obtain property for the construction of new highways or public parks. Eminent domain is perceived as a necessary power of the government.[52] The premise is that the Constitution acts as a limitation of power, not as a grant of power, where it states that "nor shall private property be taken for public use, without just compensation."[53] If the power of eminent domain is properly exercised, it provides an "orderly compromise between the public good and the protection and indemnification of private citizens whose property is taken."[54]

When Oakland brought the eminent domain action against the Raiders, the lawsuit made both popular and legal press headlines. The popular press headlines were natural; the city was so angry, it was suing to keep its team. But what prompted the legal headlines is that no governmental entity had ever sought to condemn a sports franchise. The issue of condemning "intangible" property was unique as well. Like the lawsuit by the San Francisco Seals hockey franchise, this constituted a case of first impression.

Throughout the appellate process, the language of the case focused largely on whether a sports franchise was a proper subject for such a governmental action. The concept of a person's business being taken by a city was the subject of many commentators.[55] It is often the folly of legal scholars to take the potential rule of a case and extrapolate it to its logical or illogical extreme. Here, the extrapolations queried that there may be no limit on the type of business a city could, and probably would, condemn.

Could a city condemn, for example, a General Motors plant, preventing a move to cheaper labor in Latin America?[56] California Supreme Court Chief Justice Rose Bird raised the following related queries:

[I]f a rock concert impresario, after some years of producing concerts in a municipal stadium, decides to move his productions to another city, may the city condemn his business, including his contracts with the rock stars, in order to keep the concerts at the stadium? If a small business that rents a storefront on land originally taken by the city for a redevelopment project decides to move to another city in order to expand, may the city take the business and force it to stay at its original location? May a city condemn *any* business that decides to seek greener pastures elsewhere under the unlimited interpretation of eminent domain law that the majority appear to approve?[57]

Extreme theorizing aside, the California courts initially ruled that this kind of taking is permissible under the law. The question of whether intangible property could be condemned became the key issue. Regarding that, the court noted the following:

For eminent domain purposes, neither the federal nor the state constitution distinguished between property which is real or personal, tangible or intangible. . . . [W]e conclude that our eminent domain law authorizes the taking of intangible property.[58]

The decision was based on the cases in California that allowed the eminent domain power to be exercised for the recreational welfare of its citizenry. What could be more of a recreational feature of a city than a sports franchise? The cases that most closely resembled this one involved the taking of private homes for parking for an amusement park and for the construction of a baseball field.[59] Until the Raiders tried one final legal maneuver, it appeared that the condemnation would take place, since the California statute allowed the condemnation of "real and personal property and any interest therein" in order to "carry out any of its powers or functions."[60]

There was speculation as to how this takeover of a franchise by a city would work procedurally. NFL rules mandate that the owner of a franchise must be approved by the league.[61] NFL rules aside, however, the court's logic was that if the city could condemn the stadium where the team played, then surely the franchise that plays in it could be condemned as well.[62] One possibility was that the city would take ownership of the franchise and then immediately sell it to a private, preapproved owner that would agree to keep the team in Oakland. This transfer would be necessary, as there is no provision in NFL rules for team ownership by a municipality.[63] Even corporate ownership at the time of this case was not allowed in the NFL.[64]

None of the speculation needed to be converted into reality. The Raiders' final defense was one which they had not previously raised. They argued that the Commerce Clause of the United States Constitution barred the city of Oakland from exercising its power of eminent domain over a business that was involved in interstate commerce. Arguably, professional football, as played by the NFL, is a national business requiring nationally uniform regulation. Therefore, no municipal or state entity could interfere with its operations.[65] Preventing a franchise from moving would constitute such an interference.[66] Based on this argument, the condemnation of the franchise was not allowed.[67]

As a final irony, it is not clear that Oakland could have afforded the compensation that it would have been required to pay for the Raiders had the city been permitted to condemn the franchise.[68]

Back to Oakland?

After the Raiders had been in Los Angeles for a couple of seasons, Al Davis began to contend that they had been sold a "bill of goods."[69] Davis asserted that the promises made by the LAMCC in luring the team to Los Angeles had not been kept. The promised stadium improvements, such as the addition of luxury boxes, had not materialized. Another promise had been to reduce the seating capacity and to improve the sight lines for the fans. With its huge seating capacity, the Coliseum was difficult to sell out, so television blackouts of Raider home games in Los Angeles were a regular occurrence.

Davis set the wheels in motion again to leverage cities against each other so that his franchise could get a better deal. As the end of the initial lease term approached, Davis jockeyed with a number of cities, including Irwindale and Sacramento.[70] Davis even explored a possible return to Oakland.

Irwindale, really more of a large town than a city, is known (if at all) for its motor speedway. Its pursuit of the Raiders cost the municipality dearly. Irwindale's initial allure to the Raiders was the proposed conversion of a gravel pit into a football stadium for $115 million. This stadium would serve as the new state-of-the-art home for the Raiders.

Irwindale had, however, a financing problem. The city needed time to raise the funds necessary to construct the stadium. In order to obtain an option from the Raiders, Irwindale paid Al Davis a nonrefundable fee of $10 million.[71] Irwindale could not raise the construction monies, so Davis kept the fee. Irwindale officials argued that Davis violated the deal by keeping the money while he was looking elsewhere, but to no avail. This small city of only 1,100 residents spent other monies on the project as well, including $7 million in legal fees. Irwindale also lost, while hope for the actual move was still alive, $3 million in interest.[72]

Even though Irwindale erected a billboard on the major freeway approaching town, proclaiming itself the future home of the Raiders, not all of its citizens favored its brief and expensive flirtation with professional sports. One citizen, Frederick Silva Barbosa, with the help of a public-interest law firm, brought suit to prevent the move.[73] The two causes of action he raised were that a proper environmental impact study had not yet been completed and that the use of public redevelopment funds for private purposes was illegal. Barbosa argued, "If Irwindale can give millions of dollars to Al Davis, what's to stop any other city in Southern California from giving money away on the pretense of making money for the city?"[74]

Not all of the reaction was negative. The highlight for the city came late one night on network television, when Irwindale's public relations consultant, Xavier Hermosillo, was interviewed by Johnny Carson on *The Tonight Show*.[75] In hindsight, it is questionable whether this amount of national exposure was worth the millions of dollars that Irwindale spent in order to be a player in the sports franchise game.

Sacramento was then a city with a recently acquired NBA franchise. Bringing the Raiders to the city would solidify its right to be considered a big-league city. The Sacramento offer included the payment of a $50-million incentive fee to Davis.[76] Sacramento was buoyed forward by an economic study projecting a $1.4-billion impact over a thirty-year period.[77] Sacramento fell out of contention when it apparently lost its bid to the former Raider home—Oakland.

It was an almost unbelievable irony that the city that had seemed permanently embittered by its loss of the Raiders fought so aggressively to get them back. What became clear was that many fans in the East Bay never stopped following the "Silver and Black." In fact, television and radio broadcasts and even an exhibition game played by the Raiders in their old home stadium made clear that many of their Oakland fans remained loyal.

Apparently based on this perceived fan support and memories of the way things used to be, then-Mayor Lionel Wilson led the negotiations to bring the team back. The offer made by Oakland originally included guarantees to the Raiders under a fifteen-year contract of $602 million. This offer was later reduced to $428 million.[78] The deal at its peak included a $54.9-million franchise fee, $53.5 million in stadium renovations, and $2 million in yearly income from parking and concessions.[79]

Mayor Wilson had made what perhaps was the largest political error of his career. The lack of support for his offer to the Raiders became obvious in the midst of a mayoral election.[80] Even though Wilson argued that Oakland would make $50 million over a fifteen-year period, his opponents successfully argued that Wilson's priorities were out of order and should center on crime, poverty, schools, and the recent earthquake damage.[81] Leading the opposition to bringing the team back to Oakland and seemingly loath to return Oakland to its former big-league status was Wilson's primary opponent, Assemblyman Elihu Harris.

At a heated Oakland hearing regarding the impending Raiders move, the error of the movement to bring the team back to Oakland became clear. The CBS *Sunday Morning* television program broadcast part of the meeting in a feature report, including the following comments from three unidentified voices:

Unidentified Man (at Oakland Hearing): . . . bottom line—money, M-O-N-E-Y. And you're jeopardizing our livelihood. Our schools need money. We have homeless people. But yet you are giving it to Al Davis—$600 million. . . .
Second Unidentified Man (at Oakland Hearing): Almost everybody wants the Raiders back. The issue is at what price. Fifty-four million dollars is—operations loan. What is that? Operations loan? I don't even understand what an operations loan is. That's Al Davis's blackmail deal. And for you to railroad this thing through in a staged production with sharks and all this kind of stuff. . . .
Third Unidentified Man (at Oakland Hearing): Either you give us a referendum, or we will take it to the next election. We will vote Lionel Wilson out of office.[82]

The city council voted against the measure six to zero, and Lionel Wilson was defeated in the next mayor's race.[83]

The Raiders eventually agreed to stay in Los Angeles with the following commitments from the city: The size of the stadium would be reduced from 92,500 seats to 70,000; $145 million in private funds would be used to renovate the Coliseum, including the addition of luxury boxes; a twenty-year lease would be stipulated; and the LAMCC would drop a $58-million suit against the Raiders.[84] Spectacor, the private entity that would manage the facility, offered to advance the Raiders $20 million. The *Philadelphia Inquirer* calculated that Al Davis pocketed $54.4 million in his string of stadium deals since 1982, including $6.4 million in 1984 from the LAMCC to build luxury boxes that were never built. The 1990 deal allowed him to keep that money as well as $18 million for the settlement of the original antitrust suit, $10 million from Irwindale, and $20 million from Spectacor.[85] After the recent earthquake damage to the Coliseum, the Raiders may be back on the road again. These moves set the stage for the ongoing wave of relocations and threatened relocations by other franchises. The actual value of a sports franchise to its host city was becoming increasingly blurred.

Chapter 6
The Field-of-Dreams Approach:
Baltimore and Indianapolis

> This is America and industries can move. But the difference is that Baltimore made an honest effort to keep the Colts. I gave Oakland the best operation in football and it wouldn't even give me $11 million in stadium improvements. The league will use this to say, "we told you so," but they could have stopped it if they wanted to.
>
> —Al Davis following the relocation of the Baltimore Colts to Indianapolis [1]

> We felt we met every reasonable demand he made, but the demands kept changing.
>
> —Former Maryland Governor Harry Hughes on Colts owner Robert Irsay following the relocation of the Baltimore Colts to Indianapolis [2]

There are two events in the history of Baltimore that are significant to this discussion of the sports franchise game. The first is the departure of the Baltimore Colts to Indianapolis in 1984, and the second is the construction of Oriole Park at Camden Yards for the 1992 Major League Baseball season.

The city of Baltimore suffered due to the initial success of the Raiders in court against the City of Oakland and the NFL. Precedent did not support forcing a team to stay in its present location. Further, the zealous pursuit of Indianapolis for acknowledgment as "America's sports capital" did not help Baltimore either. [3] The civic leaders of Indianapolis, realizing that there were no nearby lakes, mountains, or sandy beaches, chose sport as the resource to serve as a tourist attraction and an image-improving vehicle to spur development. [4] This conscious effort began with the formation of the Indiana Sports Corporation, followed by increased investment in amateur sports. [5] A survey conducted in the 1970s did not find that Indianapolis had a negative image, just that it had no image at all.[6] The success of the Raiders in court essentially neutralized a seemingly rigid rule from *Seals* barring unilateral franchise relocations. Some commentators referred to the Raiders' court decision as creating an atmosphere of free agency among franchises.[7]

Colts owner Robert Irsay had been maneuvering to move the franchise from Baltimore to a new city for some time. Irsay had voiced the usual complaints, primarily regarding the need for stadium improvements. He reportedly was negotiating with Baltimore, Memphis, Phoenix, Jacksonville, and Indianapolis for several weeks before he made his move.[8] But Irsay had not received league approval to move. Irsay appeared to be betting that the monetary judgment against the league of $49 million in *Raiders* tied the hands of the NFL. The question Irsay obviously asked himself was whether the league would risk another multimillion dollar judgment by attempting to bar a move by Baltimore. Irsay's view was "apparently not"—but with some degree of caution.

On March 29, 1984, fifteen Mayflower moving vans loaded with all of the Colts' equipment rolled from Baltimore to Indianapolis.[9] Press reports mention snowy, foggy weather conditions that appeared during a time of year when it rarely snowed in Baltimore. In response to the relocation, the league took no legal action.[10] As the late columnist Pete Axthelm phrased the NFL's reaction to the flight, "It [the NFL] had no stomach for a fight with an owner who wanted to sneak out of town." [11]

In retrospect, as legal scholars have analyzed the move, this was probably a relocation scenario that the league could have been successful in stopping without suffering antitrust damages. A key to the *Raiders* decision was the competition that their move to Los Angeles provided to the metropolitan Los Angeles–based Rams, not just in terms of on-the-field rivalry but in economic rivalry for fans in the metropolitan Los Angeles area.[12] By not allowing this competition to occur, the NFL was acting anticompetitively. In contrast, when the Colts sneaked into Indianapolis, there was no neighboring franchise, and so the same anticompetition argument could not have been made against the NFL. The best explanation of why the NFL did not challenge the Colts in court is that the league was nervous and the legal dust from their losing encounter with the Raiders had not settled sufficiently.

Indianapolis had made an offer that Baltimore, in the eyes of Irsay, did not seem willing to match. The Colts were playing in an old and outdated stadium when Irsay purchased the team in 1972 from Carroll Rosenbloom. Rosenbloom was not endeared to Baltimore's Memorial Stadium, and that is one reason why he entered into a complex transaction with Irsay in order to obtain the Los Angeles Rams.[13] In that transaction, Irsay first purchased the Rams and then traded them to Rosenbloom in exchange for the Colts.[14]

Much of Irsay's negotiations with Indianapolis and Baltimore was played out in the press. The key negotiators with Irsay were then-mayors William D. Schaefer of Baltimore and William H. Hudnut of Indianapolis. Even before the motion picture *Field of Dreams*, Indianapolis was exercising the if-you-build-it-they-will-come approach. Similar to St. Petersburg, Florida, the city of Indianapolis had built the $82-million Hoosier Dome and Convention Center with no tenant in place.[15] The difference is that Indianapolis was able to respond to the self-imposed pressure to avoid the reputation of having built a white elephant. The city moved forward confidently and aggressively. There was little if any public outcry over the expenditure, probably because of the way it was financed: two private donations and bonds that were paid back via a county-wide hotel tax and a county-wide food and beverage tax.[16]

The concept of building a facility to attract sport is not unique to the United States.[17] In 1929, Barcelona, Spain, constructed a stadium with hopes of attracting the 1936 Olympics. That effort failed, at least in the short term. It took fifty-six years for the Olympics to finally come to Barcelona, and at that point, the arena had to be renovated and expanded by over 30,000 seats.[18]

Jeffrey Kluger, in an article written for the *New York Times Magazine*, outlined the desires and demands that Irsay conveyed to Indianapolis: a low stadium rental rate; a guarantee of a minimum of 40,000 ticket sales per game; a new training facility, practice fields, and administrative offices; and, finally, a $15-million low-interest loan so that Irsay could pay off the debt that he still retained from his Rams-for-Colts swap with Rosenbloom.[19]

The interests of Indianapolis were simple. The city wanted guarantees that once the team arrived it would stay put. Its two requests were for a long-term lease and an option on the part of local business persons to purchase the Colts in the event Irsay should get itchy and have the desire to pack up moving vans in the middle of the night again.[20]

Similar demands were reportedly made by Baltimore—in addition to promised stadium improvements. At one point Governor Hughes and Mayor Schaefer were going to attempt to push a $23-million bond proposal for stadium improvements through the state legislature. They wanted Irsay, however, to sign a fifteen-year lease. Irsay did not see the Baltimore baseball franchise being given the same ultimatum, so he refused to sign.[21] History indicates that Baltimore, as Al Davis stated in the epigraph at the beginning of this chapter, was acting much more aggressively than Oakland did in 1980 and was probably prepared to pay the price to keep its franchises.[22]

Some factors indicate that Irsay was initially sincere in trying to keep the Colts in Baltimore. One of the drawbacks of Baltimore was a city ordinance that did not allow Sunday games to begin before 2:00 P.M. The ordinance had been passed as the result of the efforts of religious leaders who wanted sports fans to attend church before attending Colts games. Irsay met with these church leaders in a successful effort to have this time restriction lifted. Irsay persuasively argued that television networks would often refuse to broadcast Colts games because of the late hour.[23] However, even Irsay's success in lifting the Sunday start time restriction was not enough to keep the Colts in Baltimore.

A number of reports, including an interview with Mayor Schaefer, indicated that Irsay "promised" that he would notify Schaefer and give Baltimore one last chance before he relocated. There was, however, no final phone call before the Mayflower vans were loaded up on that snowy, foggy night.[24]

One issue that may have hastened Irsay's departure was not an action at the negotiating table but at the State House. Aware of the attempt by Oakland to condemn the Raiders franchise in order to keep it from moving, the Maryland House of Delegates was in the process of passing legislation that gave Baltimore the right to exercise eminent domain power over the Colts franchise. Irsay wanted to steer clear of this maneuver. The city of Indianapolis had the same uneasy feeling when it heard of the pending legislation. Irsay learned about the legislation on March 27, 1984, executed the lease with Indianapolis on March 29, and moved the team's equipment from Baltimore on the same day. The eminent domain legislation was signed by Governor Hughes on March 29.

The city did proceed with an action against the brand-new Indianapolis Colts—a lawsuit relying on the newly enacted legislation, which was filed on March 30.[25] The action was brought by the mayor and the Baltimore City Council in the Circuit Court for Baltimore City and sought to allow the city to condemn and then operate the franchise.

The Colts learned about this action by telegram. Not surprisingly, the Baltimore court granted the injunction,[26] but the Colts had already jumped the fence.

In *Indianapolis Colts v. Mayor of Baltimore* the Colts battled over whether the City Court for Baltimore City actually had the jurisdiction to enforce a ruling against the Colts. The city argued that the appellate actions by the Colts were simply attempts to avoid the enforcement of that decision, since the more time passed, the less likely a court would actually order the team back to Baltimore.

These jurisdictional squabbles led to at least one unusual press report regarding the Colts. In 1987 the Colts had a contract dispute with a player, Randy McMillan. Although McMillan was in Baltimore and convenience would have dictated that the agreement be signed there, instead it was signed in Washington, D.C. *The Sporting News* reported that,

"Michael Chernoff, the Colts' team counsel, did not want to enter the state of Maryland because of the Colts' controversial midnight move from Baltimore to Indianapolis in March 1984,"[27] apparently fearing that entering Maryland could be deemed as the Colts consenting to the jurisdiction of the Maryland courts.

The Colts continue to reside in Indianapolis.

The Lesson Learned by Baltimore

After the Colts moved to Indianapolis, Baltimore was not prepared to risk losing another franchise. The city wanted to avoid the perception that Indianapolis, with arguably few attractions other than sports, had absconded with Baltimore's "major-league city" status along with its football team. More than one commentator noted that Baltimore, by losing the Colts and barely holding onto the baseball Orioles, was rapidly moving back to being recognized only as the toilet stop on the drive between Washington, D.C., and Philadelphia.

The Orioles had played in Memorial Stadium—the same aging facility that Irsay had complained about—since 1954, when they moved from St. Louis. After the Colts left, Baltimore—and the State of Maryland—began to debate whether to build one stadium or two. One park would be exclusively for baseball, and the second would be designed to "attract" a new football franchise.

In the end, Oriole Park at Camden Yards was constructed in downtown Baltimore at a cost of $105.4 million. An additional $99 million was needed to acquire the eighty-five-acre site. The stadium features seventy-two luxury boxes that lease for between $55,000 and $95,000 per year. Revenue bonds were issued to finance the stadium, with the interest paid by the proceeds from a special baseball-theme instant lottery.[28] Supporters of the stadium again pointed to jobs, revenues, and economic impact as the key advantages. The construction of the stadium created 2,858 jobs, $54.5 million in salaries, and $11 million in state and local taxes. The economic impact on the region, once the stadium was operational, was predicted to be $15.6 million.[29] During the first season in the new ballpark, the Orioles entered a thirty-year lease in the stadium, which superseded the original fifteen-year agreement. That new agreement coincided with the thirty-year bonds used to finance the construction.[30]

The other stadium, intended for football, would be built if the city received an expansion franchise or a franchise through other means. This would be a 65,000- to 70,000-seat natural grass stadium built adjacent to Oriole Park at Camden Yards, which would be financed with public funds and would boast one hundred luxury boxes and 7,500 club seats.[31]

Perhaps the most desirable expansion franchise in all of sports is one from the National Football League. Football teams draw crowds that can fill the largest stadiums. Two cities will join the League and begin play in 1995. The leading candidates in the most recent franchise expansion included Baltimore, Maryland; Charlotte, North Carolina; Jacksonville, Florida; Orlando, Florida; Memphis, Tennessee; Oakland, California; Sacramento, California; Portland, Oregon; St. Louis, Missouri; and San Antonio, Texas.[32] For a while it appeared that the actual decision and start date for the teams might be delayed even further because of the ongoing labor litigation involving the National Football League.[33] However, all major labor issues have been resolved in the league, and the expansion decisions were reached.

As Baltimore maneuvered for a franchise with its we've-built-one-successful-stadium-and-we'll-be-happy-to-build-another approach, they were competing against a unique idea in the expansion battles—the regional franchise concept. The leader in this regional presentation was Charlotte, North Carolina. Charlotte avoided presenting itself to the NFL owner expansion decision makers as a 396,000-person city, but rather as a 9.7-million-person region—the Carolinas.[34] Charlotte is not alone in its expansionist thinking. Memphis, a city with a population of 982,000, has expanded in its presentations to become the 3.8-million-strong Mid-South Common Market.[35] In their desire to present the most marketable image possible, cities that boast of increased regional size also increase their television markets, an important selling point for NFL owners, who all share in the broadcast revenues.

Another city with high hopes was St. Louis, Missouri. Like Baltimore, St. Louis lost an NFL franchise. Its primary problem when it was the home of the Cardinals was the small size of its stadium, which accommodated 51,000 fans.[36] For the last ten years in St. Louis, before moving to Phoenix, the Cardinals played to a 90-percent capacity crowd averaging 46,000.[37]

In the end the two new franchises were awarded to Charlotte and Jacksonville for a franchise fee of $140 million.[38] The city of Baltimore lost out on regaining a football franchise.

The problems with the Colts led Baltimore to act aggressively in its efforts to retain the Orioles. The success of Oriole Park at Camden Yards has caused other cities to consider the old-style architecture of the park. Philadelphia, for one, is examining inner-city sites with the Baltimore theme in mind.[39] The new stadium at least aided in keeping the Orioles in Baltimore. Washington, D.C., Baltimore's neighbor to the south, has not been so fortunate.

Chapter 7
Washington, D.C.:
Longing for the Senators

> The franchise has to have a history of substantial losses over a long period. The stadium has to be substandard with no prospects for refurbishment. The city has to have taken some steps to indicate it is not interested in baseball and is no longer going to be supportive. And there has to be some sense that staying with the community and trying to rebuild the franchise would be ultimately futile.
>
> —Former Baseball Commissioner Fay Vincent outlining the criteria for baseball franchise relocations in 1991[1]

Washington, D.C., was among the group of cities—along with St. Petersburg, Orlando, and Buffalo—that were passed over when Major League Baseball expansion franchises were granted to Miami and Denver in 1991. When these cities lost their bids for expansion teams, several announced publicly that they were resorting to what the *New York Times* called "Plan 2"—an attempt to lure an existing franchise from another location.[2] At that time, Baseball Commissioner Vincent's guidelines for franchise relocations (quoted above) received wide attention.

Expansion may be defined as the "legitimate" way for a city to obtain a franchise. Expansion involves no moving vans in the night, rarely results in lawsuits, and avoids the drastic lease concessions that are made in desperate attempts to keep an established franchise owner happy. The primary expenditure that the expansion franchise seeker (usually a group of investor-owners) must make is the franchise fee. The individual or group must show that it has sufficient operating capital to support the venture. The owners, not the host city, make the franchise fee payment, and in 1991 the fee for a baseball expansion franchise was $95 million. The problem is that expansion does not occur frequently, yet demand for teams is always high. As Table 3 shows, if a city decides that it must have a franchise, all of its hopes should not be invested solely in the expansion option.

Washington, D.C., is an interesting city to consider here because the District has pursued an expansion baseball franchise for so long. The city actually has had two baseball franchises—both named the Senators—and has lost both. The longing for a replacement continues to grow. The first Senators franchise was a charter member of the American League. This franchise moved to Minnesota in 1960. The second was an American League expansion franchise that later became the Texas Rangers in 1972.[3] The 1971 Senators drew only 655,000 fans, not near the then-desirable attendance goal of two million fans, and the team's final home game was forfeited when fans rushed the field and tore up the sod for souvenirs. This two-time loser image has not helped Washington in its efforts to obtain a new baseball franchise.

There are other barriers hampering the District's expansion efforts as well. In 1971, when the second Senators departed, the D.C. metropolitan area had a population of 2.9 million people, and its average household income was 29 percent above the national average. The city was also, like many American urban centers, recovering from racial strife and recent riots.[4]

Washingtonians seeking a new baseball franchise have made it clear that much has changed in the two decades since the last team departed. The population has increased by one million. The disposable income of Washingtonians has increased from 29 percent to 49 percent.[5]

Despite this favorable change, a major barrier that Washington has struggled to overcome is the success of the Baltimore Orioles discussed in the last chapter. It has been estimated that 20 to 25 percent of the crowd that attends Orioles games are residents of Washington, D.C. As might be expected, about this same percentage makes up the television viewing audience for the Orioles.[6]

Another major hinderance to Washington's expansion chances has been the absence of an ownership group that could show that financing was in place. This lack of a viable single or group investor became clear when the San Francisco Giants were available in 1992 and apparently no party was able to seize the moment for the District.

As the deadline for a Major League Baseball expansion decision approached in May 1990, since there was no individual or group investors in place, an alternative plan was proposed. Washington business leader Jeffrey Gildenhorn asked Baseball Commissioner Fay Vincent if he would approve of public stockholders' owning the majority of a team. Gildenhorn wanted to involve the city government by selling tax-free municipal bonds to the public, and then form a corporation to attract public shareholders.[7] While Vincent did not discourage the plan, the

TABLE 3. Major League Expansion.

Year	Team	Entry fee (in millions)
National Basketball Association		
1961	Chicago Packers (Washington Bullets)	NA
1966	Chicago Bulls	$1.25
1967	Seattle SuperSonics	1.75
	San Diego Rockets (Houston)	1.75
1968	Phoenix Suns	2.00
	Milwaukee Suns	2.00
1970	Buffalo Braves (L.A. Clippers)	3.70
	Cleveland Cavaliers	3.70
	Portland Trail Blazers	3.70
1974	New Orleans Jazz (Utah)	6.15
1979	New Jersey Nets	3.20
	San Antonio Spurs	3.20
	Denver Nuggets	3.20
	Indiana Pacers	3.20
1980	Dallas Mavericks	12.00
1988	Miami Heat	32.50
	Charlotte Hornets	32.50
1989	Minnesota Timberwolves	32.50
	Orlando Magic	32.50
1994	Vancouver Grizzlies	125.00
	Toronto Raptors	125.00
Major League Baseball		
1961	L.A. Angels (California)	$2.10
	Washington Senators (Texas Rangers)	2.10
1962	Houston Colt 45s (Astros)	1.85
	N.Y. Mets	1.80
1969	Kansas City Royals	1.80
	Seattle Pilots (Milwaukee Brewers)	5.55
	Montreal Expos	12.50
	San Diego Padres	12.50
1977	Seattle Mariners	6.25
	Toronto Blue Jays	7.00
1993	Colorado Rockies	95.00
	Miami Marlins	95.00

National League had said that it preferred local ownership with one strong voice serving as the board chairman.[8] In fact, as has been noted, most leagues frown on ownership without one strong voice.[9]

When the 1993 baseball expansion franchise fee is added to expenditures needed in advance of opening day, the investment sum jumps to $130–140 million. In addition, an owner had to match the central fund

TABLE 3. (*continued*)

Year	Team	Entry fee (in millions)
National Hockey League		
1967	Pittsburgh Penguins	$2.00
	Philadelphia Flyers	2.00
	Minnesota North Stars (Dallas)	2.00
	St. Louis Blues	2.00
	Oakland Seals	2.00
	L.A. Kings	2.00
1970	Buffalo Sabres	6.00
	Vancouver Canucks	6.00
1972	Atlanta Flames (Calgary)	6.00
	N.Y. Islanders	6.00
1974	Kansas City Scouts (New Jersey Devils)	6.00
	Washington Capitals	6.00
1979	Winnipeg Jets	6.00
	Quebec Nordiques	6.00
	Hartford Whalers	6.00
	Edmonton Oilers	6.00
1991	San Jose Sharks	NA
1992	Ottawa Senators	50.00
	Tampa Lightning	50.00
1994	Anaheim Mighty Ducks	50.00
	Miami [Florida] Panthers	50.00
National Football League		
1966	Atlanta Falcons	$8.50
	Miami Dolphins	7.50
1967	New Orleans Saints	8.00
1968	Cincinnati Bengals	7.50
1974	Tampa Bay Buccaneers	16.00
1976	Seattle Seahawks	16.00
1994	Jacksonville Jaguars	140.00
	Charlotte [Carolina] Panthers	140.00

Source: The Sporting News, March 12, 1990, p. 46, as updated and revised by the author. Parentheses indicate present location.

deposit of $4–5 million (a pool of revenues and expenses shared by each major league team).[10] Operating expenses run approximately another $50 million or so per year. What a prospective owner of a new baseball team faced, then, was an expenditure that could easily exceed $200 million for the first year. Major League Baseball also preferred that its owners not borrow any of this money. Former Baseball Commissioner Fay Vincent at one point said, "I think it's a mistake to look at this in terms of sites and cities and demographics. It involves people. It involves ownership. It involves financial capacity to operate a team and support baseball for a period of time." [11]

As the expansion decision date approached, two ownership groups became the banner bearers for "Senators III." One group was headed by real estate developer John Akridge, and another was led by Mark Tracz, the owner of a minor league baseball team. [12] At one point the two groups considered merging, hoping to increase their chances of landing a team. They probably viewed the Akridge group as providing the majority of the capital and the other group, with the minor league franchise experience, as providing the baseball operational expertise. Initially the franchise probably would have played in RFK Stadium, the home of Senators I and II. While RFK was originally designed as a baseball stadium, it would need renovation to again accommodate baseball. Of course, the addition of luxury boxes and the accompanying features would increase the expenses by around $30 million. [13]

As the expansion decision date approached, the Akridge and Tracz groups dropped the merger idea. The league had announced a preliminary application round, with all comers welcome to submit bids. The two groups determined that separate applications would only serve to bolster the chances of a Washington group's selection as a finalist. [14]

Washington's two competing groups were among eighteen groups (representing ten cities) that answered a detailed questionnaire and made a $100,000 deposit on the $95-million entry fee. Each group would make its presentation to the committee, composed of Pirates' Chairman John Danforth, National League President Bill White, John McMullen from the Astros, and the Mets' Fred Wilpon. [15] Amid a barrage of metaphors the optimism of the Akridge and Tracz groups was clearly displayed in the press. "It's the kind of day we've been looking for," John Akridge said. "Up to now, there's been a lot of jockeying for position. I see this as the gun going off. This is when we have to run the race." Mark Tracz said, "We're anxious to get our day before the committee. Spring training is over. This is like opening day in September." [16]

Following their presentations the Washington groups continued to display confidence. "I feel terrific. . . . I think we put our best foot forward. The city should be proud," Akridge told the *Washington Times*. [17] Mark Tracz told the *Times*, "It's the kind of thing where you walk out and you feel good or you feel bad. We felt good." [18]

In the end, Washington lost out to Miami and Denver. The major reason for the denial was probably the question of adequate financing. The Akridge group claimed to have $75 million, but even that was short of the needed $125 million in franchise and initial operating expenses. [19] According to Akridge money was the key:

I must have had a hundred guys tell me, "Sorry, but my banker says I can't do this." I mean these are people you could have counted on for $2 million or $3 million in normal times. Two years earlier we'd have had no problem getting the money, but two years was another lifetime ago, economically. We just couldn't swing it. Miami had the one mega-rich owner, and Denver had the same problem we did until Coors stepped in with $30 million. We didn't have a Coors.[20]

One issue to be contemplated regarding Washington's efforts is whether the pursuit of a baseball franchise is appropriate for that region. Twice, the city has lost franchises, and it may be that the focus of civic leaders should be on development in other areas. If, however, a franchise could be obtained that would play in the existing RFK Stadium without the need to construct a new facility, there probably would be positive benefits, both economical and psychological, for the region. Not only would no new stadium need to be built, but the roads and other infrastructure are already in place.

Can Legislation Create Franchise Stability?

The major concern that the District has had in more recent years, however, has been the fate of the existing primary tenant in RFK Stadium, the Washington Redskins. Their owner, Jack Kent Cooke, announced before the beginning of the 1992 football season that he was planning to build a new stadium in Alexandria, Virginia, in 1994. Cooke's announcement led Washington, D.C., Mayor Sharon Pratt Kelly to make two memorable pronouncements. The first, in reacting to the initial announcement by Cooke: "as the youngsters would say, Mr. Cooke has dissed the District of Columbia." Furthermore, noting that she would continue to take a strong negotiating stance and that she would make no further concessions to Cooke to keep the Redskins in place, Kelly proclaimed that she would not "allow our good community to be steamrolled by . . . a billionaire bully."[21]

This was an extraordinarily tough time for a politician to take such a stance. First, this was not just any team; the Redskins were the reigning Super Bowl champions. Second, the District had just missed out—yet again—on being granted that third chance at supporting a baseball franchise. Finally, if the Redskins did leave, there would be no major league franchise playing in RFK Stadium or within the District of Columbia.[22]

Another not uncommon occurrence when there is a battle for a franchise is the introduction of remedial legislation. The Maryland legislation described in the previous chapter was an attempt to provide a city with the specific legal power to prevent a franchise from departing.[23] With a franchise relocation dispute in the nation's legislative headquarters, proposed relocation legislation was inevitable.

This type of legislation has also been introduced at the federal level. For example, in 1985 the Professional Sports Team Community Protection Act was introduced by Senator Slade Gorton.[24] Gorton made several attempts to pass legislation designed to protect communities that supported their franchises, by setting forth specific conditions to be met before a franchise could relocate.[25] In 1992 during the Washington Redskins negotiation, Eleanor Holmes Norton, Washington, D.C., Delegate to Congress, introduced legislation to keep the Redskins in the District.[26] The Norton bill is indicative of the goal of this type of law at the federal level. In many ways it is designed to do what the California courts ultimately would not allow the city of Oakland to do. The city gains a right of first refusal or, maybe more specifically, the right to match the offer of the competing party before the franchise can move.[27]

Federal legislation specifically aimed at professional sports is rare. Hearings are more frequent than actual legislation. As Donald Fehr, the head of the Major League Baseball Players Association has described it, "Essentially sports hearings are about publicity. They have not been very substantive."[28] The major legislation on the books is the 1961 legislation exempting much of network sports broadcasting from the antitrust laws.[29] The NFL lobbied for this legislation to allow that league to negotiate television contracts as a single entity and to pool revenues. Basketball, baseball, and hockey benefit from this law as well. Later, Congress passed legislation allowing the AFL-NFL merger to occur without violating the antitrust laws.[30]

Baseball also enjoys a higher level of freedom from scrutiny from antitrust laws because of a 1922 judicially created exemption from the antitrust laws.[31] The courts have basically said that because of this 1922 decision, the antitrust laws do not apply to baseball unless Congress passes legislation to the contrary.

So football, basketball, and hockey through legislation—and baseball through its Court-created antitrust exemption—all have reason to be concerned about the special power the U.S. Congress holds over them. This situation has led to some interesting interaction between the leagues and Congress on the relocation issue.[32]

Author David Harris described one such exchange when Commissioner Pete Rozelle of the NFL was seeking federal legislation in 1966 to enable the AFL and NFL to merge. The support of Representative Hale Boggs of Louisiana was essential to the passing of the legislation. Harris reports the exchange as follows:

"Well, Pete," Boggs offered, "it looks great."
"Great, Hale," Rozelle answered, "that's great."
"Just for the record," Boggs continued, "I assume we can say the franchise for New Orleans is firm?"

"Well," Rozelle hedged, "it looks good, of course, Hale, but you know it still has to be approved by the owners. I can't make any promises on my own."

Boggs said nothing for a moment, just staring at Rozelle. "Well, Pete," he finally answered, "why don't you just go back and check with the owners. I'll hold things up here until you get back."

Now it was Rozelle's turn to go silent for a moment. "That's all right, Hale," he finally offered. "You can count on their approval."

Less than an hour later, the NFL had its merger exemption. Three weeks later, the freshly merged football business added its first expansion franchise, the New Orleans Saints.[33]

Although the individual bills have varied in length and focus, legislation introduced at the federal level has been similar in providing specific guidelines that determine when a franchise may relocate.[34] As with any legislation, the bills tend to carry more baggage than just the specific purpose of regulating franchise relocation. Related issues added to proposed bills have ranged from extending the antitrust exemption to other sports in addition to baseball to removing baseball's antitrust exemption.

In principle, the concept of establishing specific rules that would apply to all of the parties in the sports franchise game seems to be a good idea. The Professional Sports Community Protection Act of 1985 proposed by several senators spelled out the specific issues that must be considered to determine whether a move was "reasonable and appropriate": the adequacy of the existing facility, the adequacy of the existing supportive infrastructure, the efforts on the part of the existing facility's ownership to make improvements, the extent to which public financial support is received by the franchise, the impact of changing the contract on the franchise as well as public and private parties, the extent to which the franchise itself contributed to the need to relocate, the revenues of the franchise relative to others in the league, the financial losses of the franchise, the level of fan support, the number of other teams participating in the same sport in the same territory as the franchise, any offers to purchase the club, the extent to which good-faith negotiations to remain in the same location have taken place, and any other factors which may be appropriate to consider.[35]

All good intentions duly noted, the most striking argument against this type of legislation is the invasion on the individual business rights of the owners and leagues. Senator John Danforth acknowledged this reality in the hearings regarding his legislation and offered the following justification:

Normally, the Congress would not concern itself with the movement of one business—a factory, for example—from one community to a second community, but a sports team is different from the normal business. A sports team is closely identified with the community itself. A sports team carries with it the support of the community, the identity of the community, and the spirit of the community.[36]

This "difference" between a sports franchise and a factory or other conventional business has not been enough for any of the federal legislation to be passed. All of the proposed bills have failed.[37]

In the meantime, the Redskins and Washington, D.C., reached an agreement, and the team will remain in the city for the time being, as Cooke openly continues to look for new locations.

Chapter 8
Putting the Pursuit into Perspective: The Value of Sports

> The franchise belongs to the inner city of Detroit; I'm just the caretaker.
>
> —John Fetzer, the owner of the Detroit Tigers baseball franchise in 1974, on why he would not desert inner-city Tiger Stadium for the suburban Pontiac Silverdome[1]

It is vividly clear that sports franchises and major sporting events will continue to be aggressively pursued by cities, and franchise owners and event organizers will continue to play one city off against the others. Cities must be willing to evaluate, in a more public way, whether the huge expenditures needed to be perceived as "big-league" are worthwhile. Civic leaders must make it clear to their constituencies that there is no bright line cutoff point that determines when to give a franchise owner more or when to back off. The decision whether to pursue a franchise or a major event, despite the influence of economic impact studies, is largely subjective.

There will continue to be increasing pressure on communities to build new, state-of-the-art sports facilities. The broadcast fees being paid to leagues by television networks could even decrease, putting additional pressure on team owners.[2] In order to maintain overall revenues at the current levels, construction of new facilities will probably be the single biggest demand of sports enterprises. As one commentator phrased it, "If there's anything happening today it's an increasing number of clubs trying to get new facilities, recognizing that their reliance on national media is going to go down."[3] The days of owners like John Fetzer, whose attitude about the relationship between a franchise and its home city is quoted above, appear to be on the wane.

The trend of municipal and state financing would be more palatable if cities could obtain at least partial ownership interest in a team after making large expenditures to accommodate the needs of the franchise. Joan Kroc was rebuffed by baseball's National League when she tried to transfer the Padres to the city of San Diego. The Montreal Expos received a similar response in their attempt to transfer an ownership interest to Montreal and the Province of Quebec.[4] Similarly, the leagues frown upon community ownership in the other professional sports. The types of returns available for private investors in sports franchises are not available to cities. Clearly, no governmental entity should be given *operational* control of a sports franchise. Too often we have seen the operational shortcomings of the government. However, an ownership interest, a right to participate in a percentage of the profits after making an investment, makes sense.

Apparently, some civic leaders have not yet fully grasped that the franchise-owner-as-caretaker days are all but passé. San Francisco's Mayor Frank Jordan, commenting on the seemingly imminent departure of the San Francisco Giants, said, "To allow a team with the tradition and loyal following of the San Francisco Giants to be moved for strictly financial reasons is to severely undermine what makes the game so special."[5] This attitude may have been true with Fetzer, but elsewhere the emphasis on business and profits appears to be outweighing "what makes the game so special."

As has been discussed in previous chapters, much debate has taken place on the value of professional sports. The beneficiaries of this value range widely, from local communities, cities, and states, to entire nations.[6] The economic, social, and emotional value of sports to a municipality has been discussed throughout this book. Discussions of the social value of sports also tend to focus on intangible benefits such as the impact on America's youth, with athletes serving as role models and sports providing life's lessons in a regimented microcosm of human competition, victory, and defeat.

Along with the cumulative activity described in this book—franchises relocating, leagues expanding, competition among host cities growing— there has been a growing debate regarding the value of sports franchises and events to various communities. These debates spawned a number of claims of actual monetary value of a franchise or major sporting event to a particular geographic region. Many of these studies have been used as the basis for an aspiring or incumbent politician's position on a "soon to depart" or "desirous of moving" franchise. Some politicians have acknowledged that the true value is not merely monetary. If a city does not have a major sports franchise, it is not considered big-league and will be perceived in many ways as second-class.

The presence of a sports franchise probably does invigorate the interest of a community's citizens, including the city's youth, in participation in a sport. Even though today, more often than not, inner-city kids and the children of suburban blue-collar workers cannot afford to attend games, television allows them to be fans.

One of the classic arguments—now often disputed—is that sports is the key vehicle for minority youth to escape the poverty and other ills of the city. If this argument were true, a financial emphasis on sports by a city, even without a positive traditional return on investment, would be commendable. Unfortunately, a relatively few success stories have distorted the amount of emphasis that should be placed on athletic careers. Many authorities, such as Northeastern University Center for the Study of Sport Director Richard Lapchick, International Olympic Committee member Anita DeFrantz, and the late tennis great and author Arthur Ashe, have observed that the odds of becoming a neurosurgeon are better than the odds of becoming a professional athlete. The odds of becoming a professional athlete are often quoted as one in ten thousand.[7]

Support for sports is important. However, sports is not the financial savior for troubled cities, and it should not be the mecca of careers for underprivileged youth. It is even less clear that expenditures on professional sports have much long-term positive impact on the youth of a city at all.[8]

The financial impact justification for a sports franchise is, at best, difficult to make. The impact on youth, particularly the argument that professional athletes are positive role models, should probably be deemphasized as well.[9] The personal and legal problems of star athletes such as Pete Rose, O. J. Simpson, and Mike Tyson certainly lend credence to this. Whether or not they should, the evidence increasingly indicates that not only do athletes not want to serve as role models, but that for the most part—beyond their prowess in sport—they do not serve as suitable role models. A 1992 study by Motivational Educational Entertainment Productions, sponsored by the Robert Wood Johnson Foundation, indicates that the athlete as role model is an obsolete notion.[10] The study finds that the impact that athletes can have is on the "hip-hop generation's" view of sports—not on social issues.[11] Athletes are the wrong people to look to for leadership on social concerns.[12] Isiah Thomas, the former Detroit Pistons all-star basketball player, told *Business Week*, "Just because a guy can slam-dunk a basketball or throw a football doesn't mean you want him speaking out on social issues."[13] Cities should not extrapolate much more from the relationship between franchise and city other than the positive, but impossible to quantify, image transformation and the potential, but difficult to measure, financial benefits, absent some other special provision in their lease arrangements or the presence of extraordinary athletes.

The voters in St. Petersburg, Florida, were not asked directly about financing the Suncoast Dome. The voters in San Francisco, San Jose, and Oakland were, and they refused, perceiving other community issues as being higher priorities. There certainly is value to having a professional sports franchise in a city, but a franchise is not a financial panacea, as was widely believed in the 1970s and 1980s. The puzzle has become more complex than merely joining the big leagues in order to make a city appear big-league.

Cities that do pursue franchises, or that attempt to retain one that threatens to leave, should evaluate the value of a franchise on two fronts. The first is *image*; does this city need an image face-lift? Second, is there a way that support of this franchise can serve to fund some specific civic need, such as recreational sports facilities? With the abundant revenue streams that flow through professional sports, it would not be unreasonable to earmark some portion of the proceeds to support related activities that would benefit the overall community.

When Mayor Hudnut of Indianapolis landed the Colts, he said, "I was saying for eight years we were in the process of becoming major league; now we can say, I think without grandiose pomposity, that we are a major-league city."[14] Hudnut was correct; from a public relations standpoint, the presence of a sports franchise is positive. If the community lacks alternative resources that could be emphasized instead of sports, a thorough evaluation should be made of an increased expenditure on the sports sector.[15]

The specific funding of civic needs was just a footnote in one of the Philadelphia franchise sagas. It was proposed that some percentage of revenues generated from these sports ventures could be directly channeled to help problem areas in the host city. If this could be done, then perhaps increased expenditures on sports are justified. The possibility of $2 million in annual parking revenues being dedicated to fund public recreation programs failed in Philadelphia, but it did raise an interesting and positive prospect.

A vivid example of the positive and tangible legacy that a sporting event can leave behind is the Amateur Athletic Foundation of Los Angeles. The foundation was endowed by sports—not by a professional sports franchise, but by the 1984 Olympic Games. The 1984 Olympics produced a surplus of $222,716,000, the largest profit of any sporting event ever.[16] A portion of this surplus ($94 million) from the Los Angeles Games endows the operation of the foundation. The goal of the foundation is not to train the youth of Southern California for professional sports. That would perpetuate the "escape the ghetto through sports" myth. Instead, its goal is to make sports available where it has not existed before.

This has been done by investing $40 million in the community through almost 500 grants to various youth sports organizations.[17]

There is a growing perception that the value that these sports franchises and events generate can be channeled more directly than the way reflected in economic impact studies, which use multipliers to estimate the overall impact of the dollars spent in support of professional sports. One of the major challenges in planning the 1996 Olympics, which will be held in Atlanta, Georgia, has been negotiations for the construction of a new stadium which will be the new home of the Atlanta Braves following the Olympic Games. The complex stadium negotiation required the Braves and the Olympic Organizing Committee—as well as the city and the Atlanta Fulton County Stadium Commission—to agree on a plan. The plan had to include transformation of the Olympic Stadium into a baseball park following the Olympics.

Community groups, perceiving that the Olympic Games will bring millions of dollars to the city, sought to be involved in all negotiations relating to the Olympics, including the construction of the stadium. Their efforts, which largely focused on the impact on the neighborhood surrounding the stadium, initially appeared to bear fruit. Tentatively, the neighborhood was scheduled to gross about $334,125, to be paid into a community fund. This revenue would flow from 825 parking spaces at five dollars per space from a paved-over Fulton County Juvenile Court Detention and Treatment Center.[18]

The Atlanta community leaders were not pleased with the size of this concession, but this community benefit, albeit small, did come about as a result of their efforts. Initially, these leaders requested 25 percent of the total parking revenues from all spaces at all stadium events. They also requested that local residents receive priority in hiring for jobs and contracts with the new stadium.[19] All they have ended up with is the promise of the limited parking space fund, which may not even come to fruition, since an Olympic museum has been proposed for construction on this space.[20] Douglas Deam, a community leader, summarized the feelings of many in the community when he said, "The Olympics get a stadium, the Braves get a new home and the community gets screwed."[21] The other parking revenues will go to the Braves. In regard to this situation and the need for a franchise to give back to its host city, stadium negotiator Peter Bynoe commented, "The franchise, as a corporate citizen, has a responsibility to the city."[22]

A similar flurry of community pleas were heard when funding for public high school sports in Chicago faced elimination due to city budget cuts. The announcement of the $1.5 million in budget cuts came two days after basketball star Earvin "Magic" Johnson signed a one-year

$14.6-million contract extension. The proximity of the Johnson contract to the budget cuts did cause many to call upon athletes again to fill the void. There were also, interestingly enough, calls for the local professional teams to step in as well.[23]

It is not necessary to view the redevelopment of a stadium as separate from the redevelopment of the inner city. This concept did not escape the vision of those charged with redeveloping the Los Angeles Memorial Coliseum in fulfillment of the city's obligations to Al Davis. Following the Los Angeles riots, Wayne Ratkovich, the developer for the stadium project, and Joe Cohen, a Spectacor official, stated their belief that the atmosphere of "rebuilding Los Angeles" probably improved the inner-city investment environment. The renovated Coliseum itself could serve as a beacon for the revival that was taking place in South Central Los Angeles.[24]

Perhaps an even clearer example of the redevelopment possibilities is the Gateway Complex in Cleveland. This is a $362-million project for both an arena and a stadium. The development is a fifty-fifty public-private venture. One of the key elements of the project is that the NBA Cleveland Cavaliers will be moving from their current arena into the new downtown Gateway Complex.[25] The Cavaliers have played in the suburbs since 1974.

There must be an awareness, however, that inner-city taxpayers should not be the sole financing source of stadium construction or improvement. The people who can least afford to attend games certainly should not have to pay for the stadium. Regional, state, and private funding should be used for this form of recreation. The scenario discussed in Chapter 3 regarding the Camden, New Jersey, waterfront shows how redevelopment can be effective.

A further example of the possible magnitude of development is the Meadowlands Sports Complex in East Rutherford, New Jersey. It is estimated that in the first fifteen years of its existence, $1.5 billion in office, theater, and other commercial development have been erected on the former swamp.[26] However, during a little more than the same period of time, the Orchard Park area where the Buffalo Bills play, after moving from downtown Buffalo, has seen little development.[27] Supervisor Dennis J. Miller actually believes that the value of the property around the stadium has depreciated.[28]

The community-based efforts in Atlanta show the direct benefits that are possible in the sports franchise game. A specific sum, or a specific revenue-generating source, is assigned to a particular municipal need. This arrangement is preferable to the guesswork that necessarily accompanies economic impact studies.

Should an owner of a franchise have to give up revenues to benefit a city? It is certainly a reasonable topic for negotiation. The 1992 trial of *Freeman McNeil v. The National Football League* revealed that, at least in football, there is little need to feel concern that franchise owners are not making enough profit.[29] A perusal of a recent list of *Forbes* millionaires and billionaires shows that there is little reason to worry about their financial well-being.[30] Even when the salaries the owners take have not reached the highest levels, other telling transactions have been revealed. For example, Indianapolis Colts owner Robert Irsay took a $13-million loan from his team.[31] There are undoubtedly some individual franchise owners who are community-minded and who support their local communities in various ways, including sponsorship of the arts, cultural institutions, and neighborhood social programs. However, it would benefit all concerned if the leagues came forward in a more coordinated and public way, as do banks, insurance companies, large corporations, and other major business concerns.

It's possible to add a new level to the debate over the obligation of professional athletes to serve as role models to the community. With the many social and economic problems prevalent in American cities today and the general financial success of the owners, it may now be appropriate to expect franchise owners to act in a more socially responsible manner. Team owners should take on a higher burden of social responsibility.

The existing image of the sports franchise owner, if one closely examines the battles that have occurred over franchises in recent years, is evolving into the picture of the "billionaire bully" that then-Washington, D.C., Mayor Sharon Pratt Kelly painted. Pressure should be applied on franchise owners to keep their teams within city limits and to specifically channel some of their financial success into a specified segment of the community or for specific recreation or renewal projects.[32] The owners cannot remain the only parties in America to treat sport as purely a business.[33]

In 1994 one franchise began to openly project the image of dislike for its inner-city hosts. The New York Yankees, in efforts to obtain a new stadium in the Bronx or elsewhere, criticized not only the condition of the stadium but also the condition of the neighborhood. One story in *New York* magazine had the team's vice president for community relations, Robert Kraft, saying about the neighborhood kids who play basketball in Macombs Dam Park near the stadium, "It's like monkeys. Those guys can all go up and hang on the rim and bend the hoops. It's a continuous maintenance problem. . . . It's a disappointment.[34]

Kraft's insensitivity in referring to South Bronx children as monkeys is at the opposite end of where the partnership between sports franchises and communities should be. The mutual goal should be a true partnership between the private and public sectors, with neither seeking a free ride from the other. Since a formal ownership interest is not likely to be conveyed to a city, some direct benefit should be. Owners should not be viewed as the guilty party in all instances, as reflected in the discussion of some of the "second-string" baseball teams earlier.[35] If a team is not adequately supported by its host city and the local fans—and therefore fails to succeed financially—that team's owner deserves an opportunity to improve the financial viability of the franchise. As the president of the San Diego Clippers basketball team described it before the team moved to Los Angeles, there was "a feeling of despair, if not desperation. . . . [I]n San Diego we wouldn't give away tickets, we lost our television contract, [and] our radio broadcasts were tape-delayed."[36]

A cooperative effort that takes the complete circumstances into account is the key. The collaboration between the city of Philadelphia and Spectacor is one example. Another example is the Toronto Sky Dome, which was built under the financial alliance of the Province of Ontario, the City of Toronto, and twenty-three private corporations. Similarly, the Hubert H. Humphrey Metrodome was built in Minneapolis at a cost of $75 million on property donated by a local businessman with a portion of the costs paid by the two tenant franchises—the Twins and the Vikings.[37] In another example of private financial support, $25 million for the construction of the $82-million Hoosier Dome came from the private Lilly Endowment and another undisclosed amount came from the Krannert Charitable Trust Company.[38]

The demands made by District of Columbia Mayor Kelly in exchange for city support of a new stadium also reflect the new interactive nature of the sports franchise game.[39] In order for a new stadium to be constructed in the District, 51 percent of the jobs had to be filled by Washington residents. Thirty-five percent of the stadium construction contracts had to be awarded to minority contractors.[40] At this writing, it is still not clear where the Redskins will end up.

If some version of two-way financial support between the host city and the franchise or major sporting event cannot be structured into the relationship, then that missing element may be enough to justify not pursuing that franchise or event through stadium construction or other financial support. Furthermore, if a city has other positive attractions that it can emphasize, the value of sports to the city's image becomes less important as well.

If the Redskins ever did leave Washington, D.C., the nation's capital would still have many other resources to promote, as well as other pressing problems that deserve support out of limited District funds. A city that pursues a franchise or major sporting event should thoroughly consider what a franchise or event is, and what it is not. An objective perspective regarding the actual, versus the possible, monetary value of sport is indispensable. If an impact study is commissioned, and one probably should be, the civic leaders should ensure that the multiplier and other components in the analysis are justified, and that the assumptions used in the study are reasonable. As Professors Baade and Baim have stated, the impact study should not be merely an advocacy piece, as has often been the case.

If a city already has an established sports franchise, there are times when it would be advisable to "bleed" a little to keep the team from moving elsewhere. Oakland, San Diego, Baltimore, and St. Louis have yet to receive replacements for the teams they lost—although other cities in earlier years have.[41] The empty stadium, the "white elephant syndrome," is important to avoid, but not at any cost.[42] The sacrifices that a city makes to keep a franchise should be made with caution. Even franchise owner Ted Turner has pleaded for reason. "What I personally think is that when a city is going to build a stadium that requires millions in long-term funding and they do it for a team, they ought to make that team, at the time they do the funding and build the stadium, sign a lease that would at least cover the amortization of the stadium."[43] A city may "bleed," but it should not "die." At some point, the judgment must be made that the increased expenditure on sports is just not worth the risk of financially crippling a community.

Building a stadium to attract a franchise, the St. Petersburg route, is a strategy that is not likely to be attempted again. Seven times St. Petersburg thought it had finally landed a franchise, but the 1984 Minnesota Twins, 1985 Oakland A's, 1988 Chicago White Sox, 1988 Texas Rangers, 1992 Seattle Mariners, and 1992 San Francisco Giants all eventually said no.[44] Even if the city lands a franchise, the expenditure on a stadium is an extraordinarily risky proposition.[45]

Cities should pursue opportunities for expansion franchises. If a stadium must be built to accommodate a team, its construction should be contingent upon receiving the expansion franchise. The city of Baltimore, both the fans and municipal leaders, seem comfortable with their "we'll build it *if* they come" stance for football. Much of the financial burden of pursuing an expansion franchise is borne by the private sector. This is where a city can initiate a public-private partnership so that the city will properly share the economic burden—and the long-term benefits—of a franchise.

If a city does seek to "steal" a franchise, the support of the state and a privately financed stadium are certainly important assets. Without this support, unilateral pursuit by an individual politician is ill-advised. The support of taxpayers, as determined by a voter referendum, is essential.

Full private financing may not be the best option, either, and it certainly does not appear to be the wave of the future. The owners of the Minnesota Timberwolves basketball team have attempted to run a professional sports franchise with a minimum of public money. Minneapolis did, however, provide the land for the arena development.[46] The owners, Harvey Ratner and Marvin Wolfenson, built an arena for $95 million and control the revenues from concessions, parking, and everything else.[47] Recently, after the two owners encountered financial hard times, they have been negotiating with public authorities whether to sell the Target Center to the community, refinance it, or sell out completely to new owners.[48] Ratner told the *Minneapolis Star Tribune* that the arena "was more costly than we anticipated. We've had a hard time making a profit."[49]

It is not impossible for a creative entrepreneur to develop a successful project that is entirely financed with private funds. In an attempted deal that fell through, Donald Trump proposed a plan to bring a franchise back into New York City. Trump was to pay $286 million for a domed stadium in the city. He would recoup his expenditure by selling half of the seats as regular season tickets and single admissions. The remainder of the 82,000 seats were to be leased year-to-year or sold outright. Of this second half, 23,000 seats would sell for an average of $12,000; 221 luxury boxes would each lease for $60,000 per year; and 15,000 other seats would lease for an average of $2,400. This revenue would total $276 million—just $10 million shy of the projected initial Trump expenditure of $286 million.[50]

Even in this deal, however, New York City and the state agreed to provide $75 million for infrastructure improvements.[51] These improvements—the roads, sewers, and other necessities for the operation of a sports facility—are a major expense not to be disregarded simply because the private sector is building the facility. Trump would also have been the beneficiary of a property-tax exemption on the site.[52]

If this fully private ownership of a sports facility could be developed, then relocations would probably be rare events. An owner of a facility, such as the Dodgers in Los Angeles, is not likely to leave valuable property behind to seek a new venue. However, vacating an arena owned by a municipality is obviously another matter.

One somewhat successful method of attracting private financing in the past was paying for a stadium through the sale of luxury boxes and other premium seats. This approach was first successfully used in the construction of Texas Stadium in Irving. However, in the problematic economic climate of the 1990s, the sale of premium seats in some areas has been difficult. Part of the financing plan for the renovation of the Los Angeles Memorial Coliseum called for the sale of 10,000 club "seats" at an annual price of $3,600 per seat. By the beginning of 1992, only one thousand had been sold.[53] In July 1992, Spectacor, the developer for the project, announced that they had given up on funding the renovation of the Coliseum by this method, and declared that "because of current economic conditions . . . there is no longer a role for a for-profit developer."[54]

A shift from the emphasis on sports is slowly occurring in some cities. Even in Indianapolis, the city that has admittedly enhanced its image considerably by emphasizing sports, the private Lilly Endowment that invested so heavily in sports has publicly shifted its emphasis to education.[55] The negative reactions to sports expenditures without constituency consent have also been growing.

In 1990, Professors Baade and Dye presented a survey in which they asked city planners in the sixty largest Metropolitan Statistical Areas, "Do you believe that stadium construction or renovation can be justified on economic grounds?" Baade and Dye reported that of twenty respondents, twelve responded yes and only three responded no. Two said they were not sure, one felt uncomfortable answering the question, and two did not answer the question.[56] Those that must make these tough decisions are not in agreement.

On the political front, there will always be a new generation of politicians who fear that they will be voted out of office for losing a franchise during their watch. If they do not lose their jobs, at the very least they will be subject to heavy criticism. In addition to negative voter reactions, there have been other forms of negative reactions by the public. In one unique example, the predominantly black neighbors of Miami's Joe Robbie Stadium filed a law suit which claimed that their civil rights were violated when a stadium was built in their residential neighborhood.[57] "It's horrendous. We feel like they steamrolled over our legal rights because we were perceived as a powerless black community."[58]

One of the pioneers in examining sport and viewing its societal impact is the sociologist Dr. Harry Edwards. In his landmark work which legitimized sport as an area for serious study, *Sociology of Sport*, he cites a 1928 book, *$port$* by John Tunis. One quote eerily summarizes the situation in our cities today:

The Great Sports Myth . . . is a fiction sustained and built up by . . . the newsgatherers [and other] professional sports uplifters . . . who tell us that competitive sport is health-giving, character-building, brain-making and so forth. . . . They imply more or less directly that its exponents are heroes, possessed of none but the highest of moral qualities; tempered and steeled in the great white heat of competition; purified and made holy by their devotion to . . . sport. Thanks to [coaches and sportswriters], there has grown up in the public mind an exaggerated and sentimental notion of the moral value of great, competitive sport spectacles. . . .
Why not stop talking about the noble purposes which sports fulfill and take them for what they are? . . . In short let us cease the elevation of [sport] to the level of a religion.[59]

The true value of sports to our cities cannot be measured. When confronted with options regarding a stadium, franchise, or event, a city's choices and decisions must depend on the complete circumstances and an objective consideration of the actual value of sports. Some of the values that are typically espoused fall into Tunis's broad category of the "Great Sports Myth." Instead of such myths, caution and true perspective must take control as America's cities continue to pursue sports franchises, stadiums, arenas, and events.

Notes

Introduction

1. July 22, 1992, speech by Mayor Sharon Pratt Kelly at Robert F. Kennedy Stadium, in Washington, D.C. ("Kelly speech").

2. See A. Zimbalist, *Baseball and Billions* (New York: Basic Books, 1992), p. 136.

3. See Rosentraub and Nunn, "Suburban City Investment in Professional Sports," *American Behavioral Scientist*, vol. 21, no. 3 (Jan.–Feb. 1978): 393. Without question, this flight away from the cities is not just a sports problem. The headlines of major newspapers often report the impending departure of one business or another. See e.g., Finder, "Offering Tax Credits, New York City Keeps Morgan Stanley Co.," *New York Times*, Oct. 20, 1992, p. 1, col. 1 (discussing the successful efforts to keep a company that will pay $911 million in taxes over the next ten years to the city and state). Id. A 1970 study found that fifty-three of seventy-three professional sports stadiums were owned by public authorities. See Benjamin Okner, "Subsidies of Stadiums and Teams," in *Government and the Sports Business*, ed. R. Noll (Washington, D.C.: Brookings Institute, 1974), p. 325.

4. One commentator writes, "A friend of mine named David, a professional making $50,000 a year, has four season tickets to the Miami Dolphins. He says when he takes his wife and kids to a game for the 'full experience,' he spends as much as $200 on tickets, parking, food, and drink. To ease the pain a little, he says, he once tried to smuggle in a bag of popcorn his wife made and had it commandeered, with a lecture, by a storm trooper at the gate." See Underwood, "Screwball," *Florida Trend*, Nov. 1992, p. 46 at 49.

5. See *The 1994 Information Please Sports Almanac*, ed. M. Meserole (Boston: Houghton Mifflin, 1994), pp. 492–93.

6. See Comte and Stogel, "Sports: A $63.1 Billion Industry; Despite Volatile Consumer Spending, Sports Economy Segments Are Growing," *The Sporting News*, Jan. 1, 1990, p. 60. ($63.1 billion was the "sum of output and services generated by the sports industry in 1988" as calculated by the Wharton Econometric Forecasting Associates Group. This was a 7.5 percent increase from the $58.7 billion 1987 GNSP [Ibid.].)

7. Baim, "Sports Stadiums as 'Wise Investments': An Evaluation," Heartland Policy Study, Nov. 26, 1990, no. 32, p. 1. The number is constantly increasing as new plans for stadium development spring up. See, e.g, "Brewers Press Plan for New Stadium," *Sports Industry News*, Aug. 21, 1992, p. 261 (discussing the on-and-off talks regarding building a new stadium in Milwaukee).

8. See Zimbalist, "Take Me out to the Cleaners," *New York Times,* July 14, 1992, A-25, col. 1.

9. See "Call Your Broker: Stocks Outperformed N.F.L. Teams," *New York Times,* Aug. 21, 1992, B-11 col. 1. The article also sets out the counterargument that the increase in value of the franchise has lagged behind the stock market. Braman's return on his 1985 $67.5-million investment to purchase the Eagles franchise, which increased in value to $125 million in 1992, is 9 percent. The Standard and Poor's Index had an average return of 18.1 percent over that same period of time. (Ibid.) Although the owners' income from sports has just recently been revealed, the presence of sports owners on prestigious wealth lists such as the one published by Forbes is old news. See, e.g., Merwin, "Dumb like Foxes," *Forbes,* Oct. 24, 1988, pp. 45, 46 (listing twenty-six members of the 1988 Forbes 400 list who held at least a 30 percent interest in a sports franchise). Ibid at 46.

10. See Richard Hoffer, "Too Hot to Handle," *Sports Illustrated,* May 11, 1992, p. 7.

11. Ibid.

12. November 11, 1992, interview with Philadelphia Sports Congress Executive Director Diane Hovencamp, Philadelphia, Pennsylvania.

13. See discussion in Chapter 8. Along these lines, when Cincinnati Reds owner Marge Schott was sanctioned by Major League Baseball for uttering various racial epithets, she was almost certainly held to a higher standard than the owner of a factory with a similar net worth and mentality.

14. See B. Woodward and S. Armstrong, *The Brethren* (New York: Simon and Schuster, 1979), pp. 189–92.

Chapter 1. The Sports Franchise Game

1. Quoted in Brown, "Scoreboard, or Profit Center?" *Forbes,* May 21, 1984, p. 191.

2. M. Harris, *Bang the Drum Slowly* (Lincoln: University of Nebraska Press, 1956).

3. It may be more appropriate from a team owner's standpoint to call this interaction the "stadium game" because that is what the owner is often battling for—the best stadium or stadium deal possible. Author David Harris cites a *Fortune* article as dubbing this interaction "promoters v. Taxpayers in the Superstadium game." See D. Harris, *The League: The Rise and Decline of the NFL* (New York: Bantam Books, 1986). This could just as easily be called the "events game" since the same types of battles take place for major sporting events such as the Olympics, Super Bowls, All-Star games, and sports festivals. See, e.g., notes 10– 12 below and accompanying text.

4. See generally Grauer, "Recognition of the National Football League as a Single Entity Under Section 1 of the Sherman Act: Implications of the Consumer Welfare Model," 82 *Michigan Law Review* 1 (1983). See also *Levin v. NBA,* 385 F. Supp. 149, 152(S.D.N.Y.) 1974 (equating joint venturers in the NBA with a partnership). But cf. Roberts, "Sports Leagues and the Sherman Act: The Use and Abuse of Section 1 to Regulate Restraints on Intraleague Rivalry," 32 *UCLA Law Review* 219, 225 (1984). As will be discussed in Chapters 4 and 5, a major legal contention of the leagues is that they are single entities and not several separate business enterprises represented by teams.

5. This is prime territory for what economists call opportunistic behavior.

Oliver Williamson defines opportunism as "self-interest seeking with guile." O. Williamson, *Markets and Hierarchies: Analysis and Antitrust Implications* (New York: Free Press, 1975), p. 26.

6. This book does not give much focus to the plight of the athletes relocated by a franchise move. This is not an oversight but a recognition of the importance of the issue and the attention it deserves. In Curt Flood's landmark lawsuit against Major League Baseball in 1972, a primary issue was the right of the athlete to have some say as to where he or she plays. The Flood case involved his trade from St. Louis to Philadelphia. Although no major litigation has yet addressed the issue, surely many of the same questions arise if an entire franchise relocates from St. Louis to Philadelphia. Flood lost his case involving a trade, but a case involving a relocation and a different sport would require renewed scrutiny, although one suspects those player actions would be unsuccessful as well. See *Flood v. Kuhn*, 407 U.S. 258 (1972).

7. See Baim, "Sports Stadiums as 'Wise Investments': An Evaluation," Heartland Policy Study, no. 32, November 26, 1990, p. 16. Wilson's support for bringing the Raiders back turned out to be the wrong side of this issue.

8. Ibid.

9. Ibid., p. 17.

10. Ibid. See also, "Olympics to Return to Asia in 1998," *New York Times,* June 16, 1991, p. 2, col. 1; "Nagano Celebrates Landing the 1998 Winter Olympics," *The Japan Times Weekly* (International Ed.), June 24–30, 1991, p. 22.

11. See "Salt Lake Raises Sights for 2002 Winter Olympics," *Sports Industry News,* June 21, 1991, p. 197.

12. "Berlin Proposes Free Tickets in Bid for 2000 Olympics," *Sports Industry News,* July 26, 1991, p. 234.

13. The first luxury boxes were constructed in the Houston Astrodome in 1965. See Corliss, "Build It and They Might Come," *Time,* Aug. 24, 1992, p. 51. According to author David Harris (*The League*, p. 25), Houston was also the site of the first "superstadium game," in which the Houston Oilers football club, led by its owner, Bud Adams, used its leverage to have the Houston Astrodome constructed for $43 million in 1962. Harris describes the succession that followed: the construction of the $126-million Silverdome under similar circumstances in Michigan, the $300-million Meadowlands in New Jersey, the $21-million stadium in Erie County for the Buffalo Bills, and the Superdome for the New Orleans Saints.

14. Just raising ticket prices helps, but keep in mind that often ticket revenue must be shared. See, e.g, notes 19–23 and accompanying text. For example, for the 1992 season, Madison Square Garden raised the price of the "best" (non-luxury box seats) from $45 each to $65 each per game. This was projected to increase revenue by $1,707,200 for hockey and $2,050,000 for basketball. The eighty-eight luxury boxes in the Garden sell for $190,000 per box or $16,720,000 if all are sold. Lapointe, "It'll Cost More to Be Close to the Action," *New York Times,* May 5, 1991, B-9, col. 2. See also A. Zimbalist, *Baseball and Billions* (New York: Basic Books, 1992), p. 56, for the value of these boxes in baseball.

15. See Baker, "Cooke Would Get Good Deal After He Pays for Stadium," *Washington Post*, Aug. 22, 1992, C-2.

16. Ibid.

17. Ibid.

18. Ibid.

19. See, R. Noll, "Economics of Sports League," in *Law of Professional and Ama-*

teur Sports, ed. G. Uberstine (New York: Clark Boardman, 1989), at p. 17–4, §17.02[1].

20. Ibid., at p. 17–5, §17.02[1].

21. Jensen, "NBC Retains Its NFL Rights, Blocking CBS," *Wall Street Journal*, Dec. 21, 1993, p. B8, col. 4.

22. Ibid. NBC will pay an estimated $880 million for AFC games. ABC will pay a reported $950 million for Monday-night games, and ESPN and TNT will pay $450 million apiece for the selected games to be broadcast over their respective cable networks. See "NBC Keeps the AFC as CBS Gets Shut Out," *Los Angeles Times*, Dec. 21, 1993, C-2, col. 5.

23. See note 21.

24. See, e.g., Sandomir, "Just How Super Are These Stations?" *New York Times*, Sept. 1, 1992, B-13, col 3; Sandomir, "Baseball Moves to Lessen Beam of Super-stations," *New York Times*, June 10, 1992, B-11, col. 1. See also *Chicago Professional Sports Limited Partnership and WGN v. NBA*, 754 F. Supp 1336 (N.D. Ill. 1991); aff'd 961 F.2d 667, (7th Cir. Ill. 1992) reh'g, en banc, denied, 1992 U.S. App. Lexis 12555 (7th Cir. 1992); cert. denied, 1992 U.S. Lexis 6832, 61 U.S.L.W. 3334 (U.S. 1992).

25. Ibid., 754 F. Supp. 1336.

26. They have come close to landing a number of franchises, including most recently the San Francisco Giants. See Martinez, "San Franciscans Brace for Move by Giants," *New York Times*, Aug. 11, 1992, B-9 col. 2. When they lost out on a Major League Baseball expansion franchise and still found themselves with the Florida Sun Coast Dome costing them $1.7 million to operate and $8 million annually in debt service, Mayor David Fischer formed a committee to "steal" a franchise. Smothers, "No Hits, No Runs, One Error: The Dome," *New York Times*, June 15, 1991, sec. 1, p. 8, col. 1.

27. Duke, "Cities Find Sports More Fun and Games," *Successful Meetings*, Jan. 1988, pp. 46–49.

28. Bill Johnson of the Florida Progress Corporation believes that the White Sox did not pit the two states against each other. See N. Sullivan, *The Diamond Revolution* (New York: St. Martins Press, 1992), p. 71.

29. "White Sox Incentive Deal Striking Out in Legislature," *Chicago Tribune*, May 29, 1988, p. 2. Other politicians maintained a clearer perspective. Then-State Representative Carol Moseley Braun said, "There's no way we can pay more when we need more important things. Hospitals are closing because of a lack of state medical money, our schools are in need of funds." See Kass, "City Facing a Final At-Bat: If Sox Move to Sunny Florida, Chicago Will Be Out in the Cold," *Chicago Tribune*, May 1, 1988, C-1.

30. At one point a class action lawsuit was filed by these South Armour Square residents. They alleged that the impact of these plans on the 100 percent black South Side Chicago neighborhood was racially discriminatory. See Gorman, "Sox, City Sued over Stadiums Location," *Chicago Tribune*, Feb. 10, 1989, C-13; and A. Zimbalist, *Baseball and Billions*, p. 129.

31. Ibid. (Zimbalist).

32. See A. Zimbalist, p. 129.

33. Berss, "Big League Blackmail," *Forbes*, May 11, 1992, p. 45. Fingerish, "CEO's Goal for Skydome: To Boldly Go Where No Stadium Has Gone Before," *Amusement Business*, Sept. 23–29, 1991, p. 12. The Sox will pay $2.50 on seats sold in excess of 1.2 million up to 2 million and $1.50 on seats sold above 2 million.

See Baade and Dye, "The Impact of Stadiums and Professional Sports on Metropolitan Area Development," *Growth and Change*, (Spring 1990): 2.
34. See Kindred, "In the Best Interest of Business," *Sporting News*, Aug. 24, 1992, p. 5. This was an ironic end to the threatened relocation of the White Sox. Two years earlier, in 1986, a stadium construction referendum in Addison, Illinois, DuPage County, was rejected by 43 votes. See Kass, "City Facing a Final At-Bat: If Sox Move to Sunny Florida, Chicago Will Be Out in the Cold," *Chicago Tribune*, May 1, 1988, C-1.
35. Baade, "Is There an Economic Rationale for Subsidizing Sports Stadiums?" Heartland Policy Study, no. 13, February 23, 1987, p. 9.
36. See Zimbalist, p. 138.
37. See note 33 (Berss, p. 45). See also Verducci, "Grand Opening," *Sports Illustrated*, April 4, 1994, p. 42 (discussing the successful opening of Jacobs Field in Cleveland).
38. Some of the expenditures and financial losses stemming from producing the Olympics have been staggering. Certainly, the $225-million surplus from the Los Angeles Olympics is the rare exception. For example, the organizers of the Albertville Winter Olympics reported a loss of $56.8 million. See Riding, "Albertville in Mountain of Debts," *New York Times*, July 10, 1992, B-10, col. 3.

Chapter 2. Impact Studies and Other Quantitative Analyses

1. Quoted in Smothers, "No Hits, No Runs, One Error: The Dome," *New York Times*, June 15, 1991, p. 8, col. 1.
2. See Wendel, "Let the Real Numbers Games Begin as Economists Gauge Olympics Impact," *The National*, Oct. 7, 1990, p. 28. *See also*, Janofsky, "Games Help Calgary Solve Hard Times," *New York Times*, Jan. 28, 1988, A-1, col. 2 (discussing the $1-billion projected impact on the economy in Calgary from the 1988 Winter Olympics).
3. Ibid. Note that the lobbying efforts alone for the Olympics cost Atlanta an estimated $7 million. See Yates, "Money Too Tough for Tradition," *Chicago Tribune*, Sept. 19, 1990, p. C-10, col. 1.
4. Ibid.
5. Ibid.
6. See E. Shils, "Report to the Philadelphia Professional Sports Consortium on Its Contributions to the Economy of Philadelphia during 1988," Dec. 4, 1989 (hereinafter, "Shils Study").
7. Professor Shils indicated in conversation that many people he consulted with indicated that the multiplier utilized was conservative. In a letter to Shils, Adams wrote that, following his studies regarding the appropriate multiplier, "the results are closely bunched in the range of a spending multiplier of 1.7 within the limits of the city and 2.6 for the Philadelphia [metropolitan region] . . . as a whole" ("Shils Study," p. 6).
8. See Hunter, "Economic Impact Studies: Inaccurate, Misleading, and Unnecessary," Heartland Policy Study, July 22, 1988, no. 21, pp. 2–3.
9. For more on the calculation of the multiplier, see sources cited in Hunter (note 8, above). According to Hunter: "Recipients of expenditures generated by events at arenas and stadiums, respend the money they receive. If all recipients reside in the local economy and respend their earnings locally, the local

economy will capture 100% of two spending rounds. Obviously, in each successive round of spending some dollars will go to nonlocal sources. . . . Studies of these phenomena are made possible by the use of econometric models or input/output models. . . . Larger, more diverse economies have higher multipliers than smaller communities because they are more likely to keep a larger portion of each round of spending." See also, Baade and Dye, "Sports Stadiums and Area Development: A Critical Review," *Economic Development Quarterly*, vol. 2, no. 3 (Aug. 1988): 265, 270.

10. "Shils Study," p. 7.

11. Ibid., p. 8.

12. Ibid., p. 1.

13. Baade, "Is There an Economic Rationale for Subsidizing Sports Stadiums?" Heartland Policy Study, no. 13, Feb. 23, 1987.

14. Ibid., p. 2.

15. Ibid.

16. Landsbaum, "Will Sports Really Pay Off in O.C.'s Economic Arena?" *Los Angeles Times* (Orange County Edition), March 15, 1990, p. 1, col. 5.

17. Ibid.

18. Ibid.

19. Baker and Harris, "Stadium Deal Called (Giveaway); Analysts View Plan as Sure Winner for Cooke, Risk for Va.," *Washington Post*, July 19, 1992, A-1.

20. R. Noll, "Economies of Sports League," in *Law of Professional and Amateur Sports*, ed. G. Uberstine (New York: Clark Boardman), §17.01.

21. Ibid. at 17.01.

22. Ibid.

23. Ibid.

24. Baim, "Sports Stadiums as 'Wise Investments': An Evaluation," Heartland Policy Study, no. 32, Nov. 26, 1990.

25. Ibid., p. 6.

26. Ibid., p. 5. A precursor to Baim's study was published in 1974. In that earlier study Benjamin Okner found that the revenues of twenty publicly owned baseball and/or football stadiums did not cover the cost of operation. The study examined the facilities in the 1970–71 season of the relevant sport. See B. Okner, "Subsidies of Stadiums and Arenas," in *Government and the Sports Business*, ed. R. Noll (Washington, D.C.: Brookings Institute, 1974), pp. 325–47.

27. Shils makes the same point as well. His studies note that sports-related taxes tend to be regressive, "that is, the poor contributed a higher percentage of their income to taxes than did the rich" ("Shils Study," p. 1).

28. Heartland Policy Study, no. 21, July 22, 1988.

29. Ibid., p. 1.

30. Ibid., p. 6.

31. Ibid., p. 8. Hunter writes, "It would seem, using the logic of the multiplier, that larger downturns need only be met by still larger public works projects, and the city would soon return to prosperity."

32. Hunter's comparison of bridge repair versus bridge construction is illustrative (pp. 3, 7). The following is the formula for a public works project multiplier:

Construction projects rely on both on-site and off-site employment. The on-site employment consists of construction workers and others actually building the facility. Off-site employment refers to the workers needed to produce the materials used in the construction project. The formula used to estimate the total employment associated with a public works project is as follows:

$$TE = E_s(1.0 + m_s) + E_o(1.0 + m_o)$$

where:
  TE = the total estimated employment.
  E_s = the on-site construction employment.
  E_o = the off-site construction employment.
  m_s = the on-site construction employment multiplier.
  m_o = the off-site construction employment multiplier.

The multiplier analysis for the first alternative, bridge repair, is as follows:

Bridge Repair

Direct Employment:	500 on-site + 300 off-site = 800 total
Labor Cost:	800 workers × $15,000 average wage = $12,000,000
Total Cost:	$15,000,000 (assumes labor cost is 80 percent of total)
Multiplier:	TE = 500 (1.0 + .3) + 300 (1.0 + 1.5) = 1,400
New Income:	1,400 jobs × $15,000 average wage = $21,000,000
"Extra" Income:	$21,000,000 – $15,000,000 total cost = $6,000,000

The multiplier analysis indicates that the total primary and secondary employment effects of the bridge repair are 1,400 new jobs. Assuming an average salary of $15,000, the amount of "new" income associated with the bridge repair project is $21 million. This constitutes a very nice return to the $15 million project but, as will be shown, is not as good as the return on the new bridge construction project.

The multiplier analysis for the second alternative, construction of a new bridge, is as follows:

Bridge Construction

Direct Employment:	500 on-site + 700 off-site = 1,200 total
Labor Cost:	1,200 workers × $15,000 average wage = $18,000,000
Total Cost:	$22,500,000 (assumes labor cost is 80 percent of total)
Multiplier:	TE = 500 (1.0 + .3) + 700 (1.0 + 1.5) = 2,400
New Income:	2,400 jobs × $15,000 average salary = $36,000,000
"Extra" Income:	$36,000,000 – $22,500,000 total cost = $13,500,000.

33. The original Shils Study in 1985 has been criticized as portraying a rosier scenario than warranted, a criticism that the author of the report states to be unfounded. See also Baim, "Sports Stadiums as 'Wise Investments,'" who notes: "Not surprisingly, commissioned studies have concluded what the commissioning bodies have wanted the report to show" (p. 13).

34. See Baade, "Is There an Economic Rationale?" pp. 12–13.

35. Ibid. See Kluger, "The Seduction of the Colts," *New York Times Magazine*, Dec. 9, 1984, p. 100. This estimate was made by the Maryland Department of Economic and Community Development.

36. Baade and Dye, "Sports Stadiums and Area Development: A Critical Review," *Economic Development Quarterly*, vol. 2, no. 3, (Aug. 1988): 265.

37. See Bordow, "Phoenix Fans Leave Cards at Gate," *Chicago Tribune*, Nov. 12, 1989, C-12.

38. Ibid.

39. See Roberts, "Raiders, NFL Begin Fashioning a Settlement," *Los Angeles Times*, March 23, 1985, Part 3, p. 2, col. 3-N. Raiders ticket sales hit an NFL record of $10,271,000.00 that year.

40. Spayd and Baker, "Elsewhere, Jury Out on New Stadium Benefits: Neighbors' Gripes, Development Problems Reflect Hardships Potomac Yard May Face," *Washington Post*, Aug. 2, 1992, B-1.

41. Ibid.

42. See Wendel, "Let the Real Numbers Game Begin." One agenda item that a newly formed organization of "Sports Commissions" from U.S. cities might consider is the development of a uniform format for these impact studies. If they all used similar assumptions in calculating impacts, the necessary comparisons might be easier to make.

43. See Safire, "The Disappearing -ed," *New York Times Magazine*, July 19, 1992, p. 10, citing Benjamin Disraeli as the source of the Mark Twain quote.

Chapter 3. The Philadelphia v. Camden Story

1. Quoted in "It's a Deal," *Philadelphia Inquirer*, June 11, 1991, A-14, col. 1. Spectrum II was originally announced in June 1991, but the deal subsequently fell through because of disagreements among the principals. A new deal to construct "Spectrum 2" was announced in February 1994. See Lawlor and Zauser, "Arena Deal Is Finally a Fact," *Philadelphia Inquirer*, Feb. 2, 1994, A-1, col. 1.

2. See Levy, "Spectrum, Spectrum," *Philadelphia Business* (October 1992): 48–50.

3. See, e.g., Duvoisin, "Bond Sale Brings City Relief, but No Glee," *Philadelphia Inquirer*, June 7, 1992, C-1, col. 6 (discussing a $474-million bond sale to rescue the city's economy).

4. Other venues have also pursued Philadelphia's baseball team, the Phillies. A New Jersey state legislator introduced a bill in mid-1992 that called for a stadium to be built in Camden to attract the Phillies. Other teams in earlier eras have actually left the city, including the Philadelphia Athletics baseball club in 1955.

5. A number of other areas were mentioned as potential alternatives to Philadelphia, but Camden was the primary opponent.

6. See Chapter 1, note 29.

7. See generally Peirce, "Governors, Mayors Are Suckers for the Big Stadium Shell Game," *Philadelphia Inquirer*, March 5, 1990, A-11, col. 4.

8. Turcol and Hollman, "Proposed Sports Arena Is Praised at Phila. City Council Hearing," *Philadelphia Inquirer*, June 27, 1991, B-1, col. 2.

9. Ibid., B-6, col. 2. See also Lawlor and Zausner, "Arena Deal Is Finally a Fact."

10. Macnow and Turcol, "Arena Deal Is Finally a Reality," *Philadelphia Inquirer*, June 11, 1991, A-1. See also Lawlor and Zausner, "Arena Deal Is Finally a Fact."

11. Ibid. (Lawlor and Zausner).

12. See Turcol and Holman, "Proposed Sports Arena," p. B-6; Macnow, "Arena Legislation Sails through City Council," *Philadelphia Inquirer*, July 4, 1991, B-1, B-4. The city also absorbed a threatened lawsuit on behalf of the "citizens" by former mayor and then-mayoral candidate Frank Rizzo. Rizzo died before being able to fully pursue the suit. Ibid.

13. See Turcol and Hollman, "Proposed Sports Arena," p. B-6.

14. See discussion in Chapter 8 regarding the "responsibility" that might be placed on these entities.

15. Ibid. Macnow, "Arena Legislation Sails Through City Council," p. B-1.

16. Ibid. However, the sixty-six-year figure is probably an unrealistic measure of the patience of the franchises since their leases bind them for only twenty-nine years.

17. See notes 6–12 and accompanying text in Chapter 2.

18. See discussion in Chapter 6.

19. Even before the Sixers and Flyers threat, Philadelphia had a history of biting the financial bullet to protect its sports teams. The football franchise, the Philadelphia Eagles, made similar noises about relocating in 1984. The city that most aggressively pursued the franchise was Phoenix, Arizona. The classic scenario existed once again: Phoenix desired a franchise; Philadelphia wanted to keep its franchise. Given this situation, Eagles owner Leonard Tose, as a good business person, wanted to obtain the best deal possible. As with the most recent incarnation of the sports franchise game in Philadelphia, W. Wilson Goode was the mayor in office. In the end, the Eagles received a lease from the city in 1984 running through 2011. A key concession in the lease was a ten-year rent deferment. "Tose Will Keep Eagles in Philadelphia," *Asbury Park* (N.J.) *Press*, Dec. 16, 1984, C-1, col 2.

20. Interview with Carl Hirsh, president, The Spectrum, Nov. 25, 1992, Philadelphia, Pennsylvania.

21. Heidorn, Sipress, and McCoy, "New Jersey Downplays Failed Bid to Lure Teams," *Philadelphia Inquirer,* June 11, 1991, A-12, col. 1 (quoting Camden County Freeholder Michael J. DiPiero).

22. Note, for example, the "slow" start of the football Cardinals when they moved to Phoenix. After twelve years of attempting to land an NFL franchise, a disappointing 51,987 showed up for the opener in a stadium with a capacity of 72,168. See Looney, "One Touchy Love Affair," *Sports Illustrated*, Aug. 22, 1988, p. 28. But cf. notes 37 to 39 and accompanying text in Chapter 2, showing the increase that occurred in the first years of the Los Angeles Raiders, Indianapolis Colts, Los Angeles Clippers, and Sacramento Kings in their respective cities.

23. See Chapter 2.

24. Baade, "Is There an Economic Rationale for Subsidizing Sports Stadiums?" Heartland Policy Study, no. 13, Feb. 23, 1987.

25. Savadove, "Can Camden Be Saved?" *Business Philadelphia*, September 1991, pp. 36, 38.

26. Ibid.

27. Myers and McCoy, "Teams, Kean Confer," *Philadelphia Inquirer*, Oct. 6, 1989, A-1, col. 1.

28. The city also received an $8.3-million federal Urban Development Action Grant to finance a proposed waterfront hotel for development. See McCoy, "Camden Hotel Grant Is Approved," *Philadelphia Inquirer*, Sept. 30, 1989, A-1, col. 1.

29. See note 1, above.

30. See "Rec Center Blues," *Philadelphia Inquirer,* June 11, 1991, A-14, col. 1.

31. See "It's a Deal," *Philadelphia Inquirer,* June 11, 1991, p. A-14, col. 1.

32. Ibid. ("Rec Center Blues").

Chapter 4. Shifts in the Bay Area, Part 1: San Francisco

1. Caen, "Black Friday," *San Francisco Chronicle*, Aug. 8, 1992, A-1.
2. See Johnson, "Municipal Administration and the Sports Franchise Relocation Issue," *Public Administration Review*, Nov.–Dec. 1983, p. 519.
3. Ibid. See generally J. Cuniglio, *The Names in the Game* (New York: Vantage Press, 1979).
4. See N. Sullivan, *The Dodgers Move West* (New York: Oxford University Press, 1987), p. 6.
5. See "Behind Baseball's Big Moves—Gate Receipts, Parking, TV Fees," *U.S. News & World Report*, April 18, 1958, p. 94.
6. See "Why the Ball Clubs Want to Move," *Business Week*, June 8, 1957, p. 46.
7. Ibid.
8. Ibid. See also Sullivan, *The Dodgers Move West*, p. 53.
9. "Behind Baseball's Big Moves," p. 97, as estimated by the Milwaukee Association of Commerce. (A chamber of commerce would probably have good reason to produce a positive study.)
10. The Browns were second to the Cardinals, and the Athletics to the Phillies.
11. But there was always the keen awareness that they were battling for fans with two other major franchises.
12. "Behind Baseball's Big Moves," p. 97.
13. Ibid.
14. See "Why the Ball Clubs Want to Move," p. 46.
15. Ibid.
16. Ibid.
17. Ibid.
18. Ibid. O'Malley apparently sincerely wanted to stay. He wanted to construct a stadium at Atlantic and Flatbush Avenues in Brooklyn. See Sullivan, "Cities, Stadiums and Responsibility," *New York Times*, Aug. 14, 1988, Sec. 8, p. 7, col. 2.
19. See Chapter 2, note 24 and accompanying text.
20. See Kindred, "It's Time to Let the Giants Go," *Sporting News*, Oct. 5, 1992, p. 5.
21. Ibid.
22. Ibid.
23. San Francisco voted no twice, Santa Clara voted no once, and then San Jose rejected the Giants. See Fimrite, "Oh Give Me a Home . . . ," *Sports Illustrated*, June 1, 1992, pp. 50–51. The tallies in past Giant votes were as follows: in 1987 for a downtown San Francisco stadium, a loss by 11,440 of the 181,450 votes cast; in 1989, 2,054 of the 173,646 votes cast, shortly after an earthquake interrupted the World Series in San Francisco that year; and in Santa Clara County the proposal lost by 3,491 of the 272,537 votes cast. San Jose is a city located in that county and at that time the city actually voted for the expenditures by 86,628 to 86,013. Perhaps this provided the final, misleading glimmer of hope for team owner Bob Lurie. Ibid.
24. "San Jose Rejects Giants," *New York Times*, June 4, 1992, B-16, col. 1.
25. See Bodley, "Lurie's Options Are Narrowed," *USA Today*, June 5, 1992, C-5.
26. San Jose, with a population of 803,000, was at the time 75,000 people larger than San Francisco. That city only recently received a professional sports franchise, the San Jose Sharks of the NHL. Certainly, the big-league image was on the minds of proposition supporters.
27. See Fimrite, "Oh Give Me a Home . . . ," p. 50.

28. Newhan, "Giants Go Down to Defeat in San Jose," *Los Angeles Times,* June 4, 1992, C-6, col. 1. This includes stadium and infrastructure.

29. Ibid.

30. Goodavage, "San Jose Voters Face Giants Ballot Question," *USA Today,* June 2, 1992, C-11.

31. Fimrite, "Oh Give Me a Home . . . ," p. 52.

32. See note 17 and accompanying text in this chapter.

33. UPI, "Group Comes Up with Privately Funded Plan for San Francisco Stadium," July 6, 1992, BC cycle (Nexis).

34. O'Boyle, "San Francisco Names Sports Commission," June 8, 1992, BC Cycle (Nexis).

35. Carey, "Cooperation," *USA Today,* June 8, 1992, C-1.

36. Hersch, "Tale of Four Cities," *Sports Illustrated,* Aug. 24, 1992, pp. 25, 31.

37. Ibid. See also Bodley, "AL Might Be Giant's Toughest Hurdle," *USA Today,* Aug. 10, 1992, C-7.

38. White, "Supervisors' Vote Supports S.F. Group," *USA Today,* Sept. 15, 1992, C-5.

39. See Hersch, "Tale of Four Cities."

40. See Chass, "Look What Wind Blew Back in: The Giants," *New York Times,* Nov. 11, 1992, B-11, col. 2. See also *Piazza v. Major League Baseball,* 831 F. Supp. 420. (1993) (an antitrust action by the group that attempted to move the franchise).

41. The cost of financing stadium or arena construction became more expensive for cities following the Tax Reform Act of 1986. The interest income exception on these bonds was limited by the act. See A. Zimbalist, *Baseball and Billions* (New York: Basic Books, 1992).

42. See Purdy, "Wind Baffles and Biscotti Won't Win Votes," *Sporting News,* Aug. 31, 1992, p. 6.

43. This statement is at least historically accurate. When the California Seals left the Bay Area in 1975, there was only a season ticket base of 1,500 tickets. The average attendance was 6,944 per game. Twenty days after the Sharks franchise was awarded to San Jose, 5,300 season tickets had been sold. Things change. In 1992, 8,500 season tickets were sold for the Sharks, in a stadium that seats 10,888. See Tom, "Fans Eat Up NHL's Return to Bay Area," *USA Today,* Oct. 10, 1991, C-1. See also Allen, "Bay Area Franchise Instant Box Office Success," *USA Today,* May 30, 1990, C-8 (indicating that 5,300 season tickets were sold within twenty days of the awarding of the Sharks franchise).

44. As the preceding note indicates, the arrival of the San Jose Sharks has also stirred up hockey enthusiasts in northern California. Ibid.

45. *San Francisco Seals, Ltd. v. National Hockey League,* 379 F. Supp. 966, 967 (C.D. Cal 1974) ("*Seals*").

46. The NHL has taken this concept even further by establishing a neutral-site game format to expose an even broader audience to hockey by playing games in sites where there is no existing franchise. See Lapointe, "N.H.L. Is Coming to a City Near You," *New York Times,* Aug. 21, 1992, B-7, col. 6.

47. See Jones and Ferguson, "Location and Survival in the National Hockey League," *Journal of Industrial Economics,* vol. 36, no. 9 (June 1988): 443; Quirk and El Hodiri, "The Economic Theory of a Sports League," in *Government and the Sports Business,* ed. R. Noll (Washington, D.C.: Brookings Institute, 1974), pp. 33–80.

48. See notes 19–25 and the accompanying text in Chapter 1.

49. See the discussion in Chapter 1.

50. *San Francisco Seals, Ltd. v. National Hockey League*, 379 F. Supp. 966 (C.D. Cal 1974).

51. 15 U.S.C. §1 (1988).

52. 81 *Harvard Law Review* 418 (1967).

53. Ibid., 430.

54. Ibid., 429.

55. *San Francisco Seals, Ltd. v. National Hockey League*, 379 F. Supp. 966, 970 (C.D. Cal 1974).

56. More on this "single entity" issue is set forth in the next chapter. The question of whether or not a league is a single entity may have generated the largest amount of scholarly debate on sports law issues thus far. See, e.g., Grauer, "Recognition of the National Football League as a Single Entity Under Section 1 of the Sherman Act: Implications of the Consumer Welfare Model," 82 *Michigan Law Review* 1 (1983); Roberts, "Sports Leagues and the Sherman Act: The Use and Abuse of Section 1 to Regulate Restraints on Intra League Rivalry," 32 *UCLA Law Review* 219 (1984); Lazaroff, "Antitrust Analysis and Sports Leagues: Re-examining the Threshold Questions," 20 *Arizona State Law Journal* 953 (1988); Goldman, "Sports, Antitrust, and the Single Entity Theory," 63 *Tulane Law Review* 751 (1989); Grauer, "The Use and Misuse of the Term 'Consumer Welfare': Once More to the Mat on the Issue of Single Entity Status for Sports Leagues Under Section 1 of the Sherman Act," 64 *Tulane Law Review* 71 (1989); Roberts, "The Antitrust Status of Sports Leagues Revisited," 64 *Tulane Law Review* 117 (1989); and Jacobs, "Professional Sports Leagues, Antitrust, and the Single-Entity Theory: A Defense of the Status Quo," 67 *Indiana Law Journal* 25 (1991).

57. 15 U.S.C. 15 1988.

58. See, e.g., *State of South Dakota v. Kansas City Southern Indus.*, 880 F. 2d 40, 45 (8th Cir. 1989); *In re Multidistrict Vehicle Air Pollution*, 481 F.2d 122, 127–129 (9th Cir. 1973); *Boisjoly v. Morton Thiokol, Inc.*, 706 F. Supp. 795, 804 (D. Utah 1988).

59. 379 F. Supp. at 971–72.

Chapter 5. Shifts in the Bay Area, Part 2: Oakland

1. Quoted in Valli, "Al Davis' Advice for Luring the NFL to Oakland," *Oakland Tribune*, Feb. 15, 1987, p. 1, col. 1.

2. At the time, many pointed to the much larger potential pay-per-view television market in Los Angeles as Davis's primary motivation. This additional revenue, much like luxury boxes, would not have to be shared with fellow owners. See, e.g., D. Harris, *The League: The Rise and Decline of the NFL* (New York: Bantam, 1986), p. 350.

3. The owners approved the Rams' move to Anaheim by a vote of twenty-six to zero with two abstentions (Harris, *The League*, p. 357). Part of the enticement to move south was ninety-five acres of quality real estate worth $25 million. The Coliseum lacked luxury boxes and a favorable seating configuration. See Johnson, "Municipal Administration and the Sports Franchise Relocation Issue," *Public Administration Review* (Dec. 1983): 521–22. See also Harris, *The League*, pp. 55–56, 252–255, for the demands that the Los Angeles Memorial Coliseum commission failed to meet.

4. See generally Harris, *The League*, where references are made throughout of the Coliseum as the "Grand Duchess of Sports Stadiums."

5. See D. Harris, *The League*, p. 379.

6. See, e.g., Roderick, "Raiders Fiasco Could Pass Ball to Private Sports Man-

agement," *Los Angeles Times,* September 7, 1987, Part II, p. 1, col 3. (This is a major article criticizing LAMCC management and the tenants it has lost, including the Los Angeles Rams and the UCLA football program.)

7. For a discussion of the impact of race on attendance, see, e.g., S. Riess, *City Games* (Urbana: University of Illinois Press, 1989), p. 248; R. Noll, "Attendance and Price Setting" in *Government and the Sports Business,* ed. R. Noll, pp. 115–58; and Stix, "Blackballing the Inner City," *Scientific American* (September 1993), p. 152.

8. Atlanta has similar plans for its Olympic stadium.

9. The planned complex in Cleveland actually brings a team back into the inner city. See Stoffel, "New Sports Complex Gateway to Cleveland," *Chicago Tribune,* April 5, 1992, H-2. This development is particularly ironic in view of the antiurban sentiments shown by some franchises in recent years. See, e.g., note 34 and accompanying text in Chapter 9.

10. The Vikings "won," moving to the newly constructed Hubert H. Humphrey Metrodome in Minneapolis in 1982.

11. NFL Constitution and By-Laws, art. IV §4.3 (1982).

12. Ibid.

13. As history has shown, LAMCC would have been waiting until the 1990s for an expansion franchise to emerge. Further, there are a number of cities that have lost franchises that are still waiting for replacements.

14. 726 F. 2d 138 1 (9th Cir.), *cert. denied,* 469 U.S. 990 (1984); see also *Los Angeles Memorial Coliseum Commission v. National Football League,* 791 F. 2d 1356 (9th Cir. 1986), *cert. denied,* 108 S. ct 92 (1987).

15. See *United States v. Joint Traffic Association,* 171 U.S. 505 (1898) (Sherman Act forbids all restraint of interstate commerce without exception); *Standard Oil of New Jersey v. United States,* 221 U.S. 1 (1911), 55 L. Ed 619 (1911) (Sherman Act should be construed in light of reason).

16. *Los Angeles Memorial Coliseum Commission v. National Football League,* 468 F. Supp. 154, 161–62 (C.D. Cal. 1979).

17. *Los Angeles Memorial Coliseum Commission. v. National Football League,* 484 F. Supp. 1274 (C.D. Cal. 1980), rev'd, 634 F.2d 1197 (9th Cir. 1980). At various times, LAMCC also deliberated regarding moves by the Minnesota Vikings, St. Louis Cardinals, and Philadelphia Eagles.

18. *Los Angeles Memorial Coliseum Commission,* 484 F. Supp. at 1278.

19. *Los Angeles Memorial Coliseum Commission,* 634 F.2d at 1203–4.

20. The NFL also brought a breach of contract action against the Raiders, seeking a restraining order against a move. See *Philadelphia Eagles et al. v. Oakland Raiders Ltd.,* filed in the Oakland Superior Court. Cited in Harris, *The League,* pp. 437–38, 446–47.

21. Davis signed the agreement and then proceeded to announce his intentions to move to Los Angeles in a March 2, 1980, meeting of the NFL owners. Raiders I, 726 F.2d, 1385 (9th Cir. 1984). The ensuing lawsuits included an eminent domain action by the City of Oakland. See *City of Oakland v. Oakland Raiders,* 32 Cal. 3d 60, 646 P.2d 835, 183 Cal. Rptr. 673 (1982) and discussion below.

22. 726 F.2d at 1385. Before the vote, in discussions with his attorney, Joseph Alioto, it was determined that Davis would tell his fellow owners, "Gentlemen, I'll take the Rosenbloom deal," meaning that he wanted the same approval that Carroll Rosenbloom received to move the Rams to Anaheim. See Harris, *The League,* p. 431.

23. Ibid.

24. Ibid.
25. Ibid.
26. See 15 U.S.C. section 15. See also *Los Angeles Memorial Coliseum Commission v. National Football League,* 791 F.2d 1356, 1359 (9th Cir. 1986), *cert. denied,* 108 S. Ct. 92 (1987).
27. 726 F.2d at 1385–86.
28. Ibid. at 1386.
29. 791 F.2d at 1359. This award was later overturned.
30. 726 F.2d 1386.
31. Ibid. at 1385.
32. 791 F.2d 1356.
33. *Raiders I,* 726 F.2d at 1387.
34. Ibid. at 1390–98. The district cited three reasons for holding that the NFL was not a single entity: First, the fear that declaring that the NFL was a single entity would implicitly grant the league blanket immunity from future antitrust actions; second, other entities that produced a product that was just as unitary as the NFL's had been found to violate the Sherman Act; third, the argument of a single entity was based on a "false premise"—that the NFL member "clubs are not separate business entities whose products have an independent value." *Los Angeles Memorial Coliseum Commission v. National Football League,* 519 F. Supp. 581, 583–84 (C.D.Cal. 1981), aff'd, 726 F.2d 1381 (9th Cir. 1984), *cert. denied,* 469 U.S. 990 (1984).
35. *Raiders I,* 726 F.2d at 1397.
36. Ibid. See also, Kurlantzick, "Thoughts of Professional Sports and the Antitrust Laws": *Los Angeles Memorial Coliseum Commission v. National Football League,* 15 *Connecticut Law Review,* 183, 206–7 (1983), suggesting more extensive guidelines, including "population, income statistics, and the number of college teams in the area." Kurlantzick also notes that Major League Baseball will consider blocking a relocation only if the city to which the team desires to move has a population of less than 2.4 million. *Id.* at 206; Major League Rule 1(c).
37. *Raiders I,* 726 F.2d at 1397.
38. Ibid. Following *Raiders I,* both the NFL and NBA issued new guidelines regarding relocations that encompassed the major factors suggested by the court. See, e.g., NBA Constitution and By-Laws, art. 9A, cited in Wong, "Of Franchise Relocation, Expansion, and Competition in Professional Sports: The Ultimate Political Football?" 9 *Seton Hall Legislative Journal* 1 (1985) at 55, n. 190.
39. *Raiders II,* 791 F.2d at 1360.
40. Ibid. at 1366.
41. Ibid. at 1374.
42. Ibid.
43. Ibid. at 1361.
44. Ibid. at 1361–63.
45. Ibid. at 1371.
46. 815 F. 3d 562 (9th Cir), *Cert. dismissed,* 108 S. Ct. 362 (1987) (*"Clippers"*).
47. Ibid. at 563.
48. Ibid.
49. Cardozo and Mishkin, "Does a League Have the Right to Determine Where Teams Play?" *National Law Journal,* Nov. 30, 1987, p. 24, col. 1.
50. See Eskenazi, "NFL Votes to Approve Cardinals Move West," *New York Times,* March 16, 1988, B-9, col. 3.
51. *State v. Milwaukee Braves,* 31 Wis. 2d 699, 731, 144 N.W. 2d 117–18 1986. But

see *City of New York v. New York Jets Football Club*, 90 Misc. 2d 311, 394 N.Y.S.2d 799 (1977); and *HMC Management v. New Orleans Basketball Club*, 375 So. 2d 712 (1979). See also Harris, *The League*, p. 584.

52. See, generally, *Nichols on Eminent Domain*, §1.14[2] (3rd ed. 1980).

53. U.S. Const. Amend. V.

54. *City of Oakland v. Oakland Raiders*, 32 Cal.3d 60,64, 646 P.2d 835, 838, 183 Cal. Rptr. 673, 676 (1982).

55. See, e.g., Wong, "Of Franchise Relocation, Expansion, and Competition in Professional Sports: The Ultimate Political Football?" 9 *Seton Hall Legislative Journal* 1 (1985); and York, "The Professional Sports Community, Protection Act: Congress' Best Response to *Raiders*," 38 *Hastings Law Journal* 345 (1987).

56. In fact, there was an eminent domain case that involved the taking of property for an automobile manufacturer to prevent it from leaving a Michigan city. See Note, "Public Use in Eminent Domain: Are There Limits After Oakland Raiders and Poletown?" 20 *California Western Law Review* 82, 103 (1983).

57. 32 Cal. 3d at 77, 646 P.2d at 845, 183 Cal Rptr. at 683–84 (emphasis in original).

58. 32 Cal. 3d 60, 68.

59. See *City of Anaheim v. Michel*, 259 Cal. App. 2d 835, 839, 66 Cal Rptr. 543, 546 (1968) (parking), and *City of Los Angeles v. Superior Court*, 51 Cal. 2d 423, 434, 333 P.2d 745, 751 (1959) (baseball field).

60. See Cal. Gov't Code §37350.5 (West, 1988): "A city may acquire by eminent domain any property necessary to carry out any of its powers or functions"; and Cal. Civ. Proc. §1235.170 (West, 1982): " 'Property' includes real and personal property and any interest therein."

61. See, e.g., "The National Football League's Ban on Corporate Ownership: Violating Antitrust to Preserve Traditional Ownership—Implications Arising From William H. Sullivan's Antitrust Suit," *Seton Hall Journal of Sport Law*, 2 (1992): 175.

62. See 32 Cal. 3d at 72, City at 72, 646 P.2d at 842, 183 Cal. Rptr. at 681.

63. Major League Baseball has made it clear that ownership by a municipality will not be allowed. In separate instances both the San Diego Padres and Montreal Expos were not allowed to enter into any type of municipal ownership arrangement. See A. Zimbalist, *Baseball and Billions* (New York: Basic Books, 1992), pp. xvii, 138.

64. See, e.g., "The National Football League's Ban on Corporate Ownership: Violating Antitrust to Preserve Traditional Ownership—Implications Arising from William H. Sullivan's Antitrust Suit," p. 175; "Corporately Yours," *Sports Illustrated*, June 3, 1991, p. 15. The Green Bay Packers are held in a corporate manner but are essentially an anomaly in the league, with the shareholders having no actual decision-making power.

65. 174 Cal. App. 3d 414, 220 Cal. Rptr. 153 (1985), *cert. denied*, 106 S. Ct. 3300 (1986).

66. This argument was based largely on *Partee v. San Diego Chargers Football Co.*, 34 Cal 3d 378, 668 P.2d 674, 194 Cal. Rptr. 367 (1983). There, the California Supreme Court held that state antitrust laws would illegally burden interstate commerce if applied to the NFL, noting the need for national, uniform regulation of the business of football. *Id.* at 678–79.

67. Two years later, the United States Supreme Court ruled in *CTS Corp. v. Dynamics Corp. of America*, 481 U.S. 69 (1987), that neither federal securities nor other federal laws preempt the application of legislation enacted by the state

to deal with corporate takeover bids within the state. Curiously, this case might have been used to support the initial ruling favoring the City of Oakland.

68. For a discussion of the "politics" in this area of the law see, "Property Gains," *Wall Street Journal,* July 1, 1992, A-14. See also Dunlap, "Resolving Property Takings," *New York Times,* Aug. 23, 1992, §10 at p. 1, col. 3.

69. The movement of teams in and out of Los Angeles was not a new occurrence. See Herbert, "Merely Another Face in the Franchise Crowd," *Los Angeles Times,* March 13, 1990, C-5, col. 5 (discussing the movement of teams in and out of Los Angeles since 1926). The citizens of Los Angeles did not seem particularly distressed over a potential move either. In a *Los Angeles Times* poll, when asked if they would be upset if the Raiders moved, 83 percent of the 1,901 residents surveyed said no. See Decker, "Most Want Coliseum Saved and Wouldn't Miss Raiders," *Los Angeles Times,* Feb. 12, 1990, A-1. Oakland citizens were only slightly more interested in the Raiders moving north. In an *Oakland Tribune* survey, 59 percent of the residents surveyed felt that it was "not important" to bring the Raiders back. See Reich, "L.A. Vows to Search for a Team to Replace Raiders," *Oakland Tribune* (Southland ed.), March 14, 1990, A-1, col. 5.

70. See, e.g., Chang, "Irwindale: A Little City's Big Dreams Turn Sour; Raiders: Residents, Hoping to Lure Pro Football to San Gabriel Valley, Now Feel They Were Used by Al Davis to Get Better Offers from Los Angeles, Oakland and Sacramento," *Los Angeles Times,* Jan. 28, 1990, B-1, col 5.

71. Ibid.

72. Ibid.

73. See Hudson, "One Man Takes the Field in an Attempt to Block the Raiders," *Los Angeles Times,* July 17, 1988, San Gabriel Valley Section, Pt. 9, p. 1, col. 1.

74. Ibid.

75. See note 70.

76. Hudson, "One Man Takes the Field."

77. See Hazlett, "Raiders of the Lost Park," *Wall Street Journal,* Sept. 14, 1989, A-20. The author indicates that the study assumed a ticket price for the Sacramento Raiders 30 percent higher than that of the San Francisco 49ers.

78. Gross, "Raiders Now Find Welcome Mat Thin," *New York Times,* April 13, 1990, A-8, col. 6.

79. George, "Raiders Planning Return to Oakland," *New York Times,* March 13, 1990, D-25, col. 6.

80. See Jacobs and Zamora, "Wilson Struggling to Make Oakland Mayoral Runoff," *Los Angeles Times,* June 6, 1990, A-24, col. 1.

81. Ibid.

82. *Sunday Morning,* Transcript, no. 588, May 20, 1990, pp. 16 and 17.

83. In a similar scenario concerning the construction of a stadium for a class A (minor league) baseball team, the two-term mayor of South Bend, Indiana, lost his job as well. See Baines, "Class A Controversy," *Chicago Tribune,* July 26, 1987, §10, p. 10.

84. See "Raiders Sign Deal to Stay in Los Angeles," *New York Times,* Sept. 12, 1990, D-27, col. 2.

85. Ordine, "Some Costly Coaching Blunders," *Philadelphia Inquirer,* Sept. 16, 1990, E-6. The "advance" from Spectacor of $20 million, or at least a portion of it, was evidently contingent on whether Spectacor moved forward with the project. Because of a lack of financing, the *Los Angeles Times* reported that Spectacor was not going to go forward with the promised construction and that Al

Davis would be able to keep $10 million of the monies advanced. According to the *Times*, "Neither Spectacor nor the Raiders would comment on the reputed forfeiture, but neither denied it." See Reich, "Firm Gives Up on Renovating L.A. Coliseum," *Los Angeles Times*, Aug. 26, 1992, A-1, col 4. Further haunting the permanence of this deal is the requirement of an environmental impact report for the Coliseum renovations. If this is not produced, the Raiders may be on the road again. See Hudson, "Raiders: It's as If They Never Left," *Los Angeles Times*, Sept. 12, 1990, C-1, col 6.

Chapter 6. The Field-of-Dreams Approach

1. Quoted in Axthelm, "The Colts: A Cause For Anger," *Newsweek*, April 9, 1984, p. 105.
2. Quoted in Thomas, "Colts Move to Indianapolis Announced," *New York Times*, Mar. 30, 1984, p. 23, col. 2.
3. See, e.g., "Larger Small Cities; Salvation through Sport," *The Economist* (U.K. edition), June 10, 1989, p. 49. The battle was to be no longer referred to as "Indianoplace."
4. Ibid.
5. Ibid.
6. Macnow, "Cities Get into the Game," *Nation's Business*, Nov. 1989, p. 48.
7. The view was probably expressed most haltingly in 1988 when the St. Louis Cardinals relocated to Phoenix. Even though that move was made with league approval, the owners contended that the court rulings left them no other choice. See "NFL Votes to Approve Cardinals Move West," *New York Times*, March 16, 1988, B-9, col 3.
8. See Thomas, "Colts Move," p. A-27 and D. Harris, *The League: The Rise and Decline of the NFL* (New York: Bantam, 1986), p. 397. These are the offers Irsay considered most seriously, and of all of the offers, only Indianapolis offered a new stadium.
9. See Harris, *The League*, p. 602. Irsay had reportedly told a Phoenix, Arizona, official to reserve five Mayflower moving vans before the transaction fell through.
10. Axthelm, "The Colts: A Cause for Anger," p. 105. Attner, "The Battle of Baltimore," *Sporting News*, September 28, 1987, p. 9.
11. Ibid. ("The Colts: A Cause for Anger"). According to Commissioner Rozelle: "We had to leave it in his [Irsay's] hands because of the judgment in L.A." Harris, *The League*, p. 604.
12. See *Los Angeles Memorial Coliseum Comm.*, 726 F.2d at 1390. Contrast this with the concerns of the *Harvard Law Review* article cited in note 54 of Chapter 4, in which the focus was on the illegality of restraining competition in virgin territory rather than locations with existing franchises.
13. In an earlier transaction in 1953, Rosenbloom moved one of the former Dallas Texans franchises to Baltimore. An original Colt franchise folded in Baltimore in 1951. See Thomas, "Colts' Move to Indianapolis Is Announced," *New York Times*, March 30, 1984, A-23, A-27.
14. Kluger, "The Seduction of the Colts," *New York Times Magazine*, Dec. 9, 1984, p. 102; Harris, *The League*, p. 50.
15. See Kluger, "Seduction of the Colts," p. 104.
16. Csolak, "A Tale of Two Stadiums," *St. Louis Business Journal*, March 25, 1991, vol. 11, no. 27, p. 1A.

17. It is worth noting that the construction of facilities, particularly of temporary facilities for the Winter Games, has not gone without attack from environmentalists. See, e.g., Wells, "Use of Disposable Facilities for Games Drawing Fire from Environmentalists," *Wall Street Journal*, Feb. 19, 1992, A-11, col. 2 (in which the Rhône Alps Federation presents a list of environmental problems with the Winter Games held in Albertville, France, including allegations that "a new freeway was hastily pushed through fragile wetlands and forests without regard for environmental impacts; new ski runs were bulldozed across unspoiled high-altitude alpine meadows, ignoring existing alternatives; gargantuan ski-jumping areas, bobsled and luge runs, and parking lots have been carved into mountain sides where the geology is known to be unstable; and towering office and condominium complexes have been thrown up in villages and forests where they are out of character with their surroundings" [ibid.]).

18. Moseley, "Built for '36 Olympics, Stadium Had Long Wait," *Philadelphia Inquirer*, Nov. 24, 1991, R-5, col. 1.

19. Kluger, "Seduction of the Colts," p. 104.

20. Ibid.

21. See Harris, *The League*, p. 478.

22. See note 1 above.

23. Kluger, "Seduction of the Colts," p. 106.

24. See, e.g., Thomas, "Colts' Move to Indianapolis Is Announced," *New York Times*, March 30, 1984, p. 24, col. 2. A similar complaint of the lack of one last chance would later be made by San Francisco Mayor Frank Jordan.

25. See *Indianapolis Colts v. Mayor and City Council of Baltimore*, 741 F.2d 954 (1984) at 955.

26. 741 F.2d 955.

27. "Colts Reach Compromise," *Sporting News*, July 27, 1987, p. 38, col. 1.

28. See Valentine, "Residents Worry Oriole Park Won't Be Friendly Neighbor," March 30, 1992, *Washington Post*, C-1; Potts, "It's Built, The People Will Come—but Questions Linger; Dream Field Soon Open to Respond," *Washington Post* March 8, 1992, D-4.

29. See Spangler, "O's Sign 30-Year Lease to Play in Camden Yards," *Washington Times*, Sept. 3, 1991, D-5.

30. "Aiming For '94: The Background on the Bidders," *USA Today*, March 12, 1992, C-11.

31. Ibid.

32. Ibid.

33. See, e.g., Dodd, "Free-Agency Dispute Far from Settled," *USA Today*, Sept. 11, 1992, C-1, col. 5.

34. See "Mid-Size Cities Blitz NFL for New Franchise," *American Demographics*, Jan. 1992, p. 9.

35. Ibid.

36. See "Aiming for '94: The Background on the Bidders," C-11.

37. Ibid.

38. See Litsky, "N.F.L. Expansion Surprise: Jacksonville Jaguars," *New York Times*, Dec. 1, 1993, B-13, col. 3.

39. See McCoy, "Luring Phils Downtown? Rendell Pursues Talks," *Philadelphia Inquirer*, Oct. 9, 1992, A-1, col. 1 (describing discussions between Phillies owners and city officials on joint construction of a ballpark modeled after Oriole Park at Camden Yards).

Chapter 7. Washington, D.C.: Longing for the Senators

1. Quoted in Chass, "Expansion Losers Turn to Unlikely Plan 2," *New York Times,* June 12, 1991, B-9, col. 2.
2. Ibid.
3. See S. Cuniglio, *The Names in the Game* (New York: Vantage Press, 1979), 11 and 12.
4. Cohn, "Washington Area Not the Same as Senators' Home," *Washington Post,* Sept. 19, 1990, F-9.
5. Ibid. The D.C. metropolitan area represented the ninth-largest Arbitron-rated television market (Denver, the closest competitor in the expansion lottery, was a distant fourteenth). The nation's capital is also rich in baby boomers, who make up 55 percent of U.S. baseball fans. Eighteen percent of the adult population in Washington attended a professional baseball game in 1989.
6. Berkowitz, "Washington Sizes Up Expansion Competition," *Los Angeles Times,* Sept. 9, 1990, C-9. This number is probably larger, with the opening of Baltimore's new ballpark with direct rail access from Washington, D.C. This was not the first time that the baseball fortunes of Washington and Baltimore had been intertwined. Clark Griffith, owner of the original Washington Senators, did not oppose the transfer of the St. Louis Browns to Baltimore in 1953. Nor did the Orioles oppose the addition of an expansion team in Washington in 1961 after the Senators moved to Minnesota.
7. Hardie, "D.C. Ownership Plan Submitted to Baseball," *Washington Times,* May 17, 1990, D-5.
8. Ibid.
9. See, e.g., "The National Football League's Ban on Corporate Ownership: Violating Antitrust to Preserve Traditional Ownership Implications Arising from William H. Sullivan's Antitrust Suit," 2 *Seton Hall Journal of Sport Law* 175 (1992); and "Corporately Yours," *Sports Illustrated,* June 3, 1991, p. 15.
10. Boeak and Dodd, "Expansion Fees Soar out of the Park: Ten Cities Go to Bat for Franchise," *USA Today,* April 14, 1990, C-1.
11. Ibid.
12. Heller, "Area Groups Encouraged after Pitches," *Washington Times,* Sept. 20, 1990, D-1.
13. See note 6, above.
14. Actually, the reasons for the disintegration of a unified front may have been less high-minded. Merger talks between the two groups may have reached an acrimonious impasse over the issue of stadium location. The Akridge group wanted to convert RFK to a baseball stadium, while the Tracz group planned to use RFK only temporarily, while building a new stadium in northern Virginia. See note 12, above. Both groups had strong and viable, yet totally different, concepts.
15. Berkowitz, "Expansion Groups State Cases Today," *Washington Post,* Sept. 19, 1990, F-1.
16. Ibid.
17. See note 12, above.
18. Ibid.
19. See Justice, "Baseball in Washington: Money Never Talked," *Washington Post,* March 31, 1992, E-1.
20. Ibid.
21. "Kelly Speech" (Introduction, note 1, above).

22. State support of the Alexandria stadium was subsequently killed by the Virginia State Legislature. Governor Douglas Wilder's planned financing of the project did not gain support to some extent because public money was to be drawn from pension funds. See, e.g., "Redskins Drop Stadium Plan, Negotiate RFK Expansion," *Sports Industry News*, Oct. 16, 1992, p. 327; Bates, "Deal's Demise Brings Hope to One City, Joy to Another; Alexandrians Elated by Success of Effort to Defeat Stadium," *Washington Post*, Oct. 15, 1992, B-1.

23. See notes 25–27 and accompanying text in Chapter 6.

24. S. 287, 99th Cong., 1st Sess. (1985).

25. For earlier legislation, see S. 2505, 98th Cong., 2d Sess. (1984); S. Rep. No. 592, 98th Cong 2d Sess. (1984).

26. Norton's legislation would require teams to give local governments notice before they move and also give the cities the final option to buy the franchise to keep them in town. See 1992 H.R. 5713, 102 Cong. 2nd Sess., July 29, 1992. at §2 (a) (1) and (3). See also Milloy, "In This War, All's Not Fair," *Washington Post*, Aug. 2, 1992, B-1.

27. Ibid. at §2 (a) (3).

28. Speech by Donald Fehr to the First Annual Sports Dollars and Sense Conference sponsored by the National Sports Law Institute, Oct. 23, 1992, Milwaukee, Wisconsin.

29. 15 U.S.C.A. 1291 (1982).

30. Ibid.

31. See *Federal Baseball Club of Baltimore, Inc. v. National League of Professional Baseball Clubs*, 259 U.S. 200 (1922).

32. See, e.g., Chass, "A Senator Confronts Baseball," *New York Times*, Nov. 4, 1992, B-24 (discussing Florida Senator Connie Mack's threat to challenge baseball's exemption to the antitrust laws if Major League Baseball fails to approve the relocation of the San Francisco Giants to St. Petersburg, Florida).

33. See D. Harris, *The League: The Rise and Decline of the NFL* (New York: Bantam, 1986), p. 17.

34. Not surprisingly, in addition to the Norton bill, introduced by the representative of Washington, D.C., the sponsors of most of the bills in the 1980s represented states that had lost, were about to lose, or desired a franchise. These politicians included Senator Arlen Specter of Pennsylvania (Philadelphia Eagles), Representative Ron Dellums of California (Oakland Raiders), Senator Slade Gorton of Washington (Seattle Mariners), and Senators Eagleton and Danforth of Missouri (St. Louis Cardinals).

35. See S. 259, 99th Cong., 1st Sess. 1985.

36. Professional Sports Community Protection Act of 1985. Hearings on S. 259 and S. 287 Before the Senate Committee on Commerce, Science and Transportation, 99th Cong., 1st Sess. 1 (1985) (opening statement of Senator John Danforth).

37. For a thorough discussion of the bills in the 1980s, see, generally, York, "The Professional Sports Community Protection Act: Congress' Best Response to Raiders?" 38 *Hastings Law Journal* 345 (1987).

Chapter 8. Putting the Pursuit into Perspective: The Value of Sports

1. Quoted in "Shils Study," p. 45. Fetzer also reportedly said, in reference to the possibility of moving the Tigers from inner-city Detroit, "It would be the end

of midtown Detroit." See J. Markham and P. Teplitz, *Baseball, Economics and Public Policy* (Lexington, Mass.: Lexington Books, 1982), p. 28.

2. See, e.g., Berss, "Big League Blackmail," *Forbes*, May 11, 1992, p. 45 (noting that CBS had found it necessary to "write off" $443 million from their $1.06-billion Major League Baseball contract); Domowitch, "Down The Tubes," *Philadelphia Daily News*, April 1, 1992, p. 74 (quoting several experts as acknowledging that it will be difficult for the networks to continue to pay more).

3. Michael Megna of American Appraisal Associates, quoted in Ozanian and Taub, "Big Leagues, Bad Business," *Financial Weekly*, July 7, 1992, pp. 34, 39.

4. See, e.g., A. Zimbalist, *Baseball and Billions* (New York: Basic Books, 1992), pp. 41, 182.

5. Quoted in Kindred, "It's Time to Let the Giants Go," *Sporting News*, Oct. 5, 1992, p. 5.

6. The 1964 Tokyo Olympics were viewed as a sort of "coming-out party" for postwar Japan. This was also the case for the Seoul Olympics and Korea in 1988.

7. See, e.g., R. Berry, W. Gould, and P. Staudohar, *Labor Relations in Professional Sports* (Dover, Mass.: Auburn House, 1986) (noting that of 570,000 boys who will play high school basketball in a given year, only fifty—or 0.009 percent—will make it to the NBA). Ibid. at 14.

8. There are strong arguments for and against the value of, for example, high school sports and whether or not their presence at least encourages the youths to attend school. See, e.g., Rhoden, "For Chicago High School Sports, a Crash Course in Survival," *New York Times*, Oct. 10, 1992, sec. 1, p. 29, col. 2 (citing Florence Cox, president of the Chicago School Board, who remarked, "A lot of kids do come to school simply because of sports. If the only way to get kids to come to school is through a sports program, then you ought to provide it. At least you get kids in school" [ibid.]).

9. See, e.g., Stodghill and Harris, "Black Athletes Could Be Heroic Outside the Arena, Too," *Business Week*, June 29, 1992, p. 42.

10. See, generally, "The MEE Report: Reaching the Hip-Hop Generation," Research Division of MEE Productions, Inc., Philadelphia, 1992.

11. Similarly, politicians are respected for their views on politics, musicians regarding music, athletes regarding athletics, etc.

12. "MEE Report," p. viii.

13. See note 9.

14. Quoted in Lancaster, "Tale of Two Cities: Why Football Mesmerizes Baltimore, Indianapolis," *Wall Street Journal*, Jan. 24, 1986, Sec. 2, B-27.

15. On the other hand, Professor Baim has noted that the presence of a sports franchise can bring out some of the worst in a city, adding some negative aspects to a city's image. There is an apparent increase in crime associated with the presence of large sporting events. In cities that have populations between 750,000 and two million and a major sports facility, there are "statistically significant" higher levels of crime than in similar cities without major sports facilities. One police chief explained the increase in crime by saying, "Professional basketball and other major sporting events invariably lead to a high degree of emotional fan involvement. More frequently than ever before the actions by fans require police intervention." See Landsbaum, "Will Sports Really Pay Off in O.C.'s Economic Arena?" *Los Angeles Times* (Orange County edition), March 15, 1990, p. 1, col. 5.

16. See K. Reich, *Making It Happen* (Santa Barbara, Calif.: Capra Press, 1987), p. 87.

17. See, generally, "Serving Youth Through Sports" (a publication of the Amateur Athletic Foundation of Los Angeles), June 1992.

18. Hiskey, "Neighbors Unhappy with Stadium Deal," *Atlanta Constitution*, July 3, 1992, A-6.

19. Ibid.

20. See, e.g., Fish, "Officials Promote City for Olympic Centennial Museum," *Atlanta Constitution*, Oct. 24, 1992, B-6.

21. Ibid.

22. Telephone interview with Peter C. Bynoe, December 10, 1992.

23. See Swift, "A Pro Vote for School Sports," *Sports Illustrated*, Oct. 12, 1992, p. 80.

24. Reich, "Coliseum Renovations Scaled Back," *Los Angeles Times*, May 22, 1992, B-1, col. 2. But see notes 53–54 below and accompanying text regarding the collapse of the Coliseum renovation program.

25. See Viuker, "It's Boom Time for the Playing Fields Across the Country," *New York Times*, Oct. 25, 1992, F-12.

26. Spayd and Baker, "Elsewhere, Jury Out on New Stadium Benefits: Neighbors' Gripes, Development Problems Reflect Hardships Potomac Yard May Face," *Washington Post*, Aug. 2, 1992, B-1.

27. Ibid.

28. Ibid.

29. 790 F. Supp. 871 (1992). See Klein, "Football Players and Owners Do Battle," *Wall Street Journal*, July 17, 1992, A-10, col. 1.

30. See, e.g., "The Forbes Four Hundred," *Forbes*, Oct. 19, 1992, p. 92.

31. "Trial Focuses On Owners' Salaries," *New York Times*, July 8, 1992, B-11, col. 1.

32. Politicians have lost perspective from other standpoints as well. When Los Angeles Mayor Tom Bradley ran for governor of California in the midst of the NFL trial with the Raiders, he told an Oakland-area audience, "I'm not here to pirate away a team from any city," noting that he would ask Commissioner Rozelle to "get an expansion team down in Los Angeles and leave your Raiders alone." D. Harris, *The League: The Rise and Decline of the NFL* (New York: Bantam, 1986), p. 508.

33. One league-wide project currently being explored by the NFL would financially aid high school programs. Details are not available at present, but it certainly seems to be a positive concept. See George, "Courtroom Is Venue of Choice for Owners," *New York Times*, Oct. 22, 1992, B-16, col. 1.

34. See Bai, "Yankee Imperialism," *New York*, July 25, 1994, pp. 30, 35.

35. See note 10 and accompanying text in Chapter 4.

36. Lancaster, "Hoop Headaches: L.A. Clippers Show Perils of Owning Pro Team" *Wall Street Journal*, April 17, 1987, §2, at 18 col. 4.

37. See "Shils Study," p. 46.

38. Baade, "Is There an Economic Rationale for Subsidizing Sports Stadiums?" Heartland Policy Study, no. 13, Feb. 23, 1987, p. 3. See also Csolak, "A Tale of Two Stadiums," *St. Louis Business Journal*, March 25, 1991, A-1.

39. Others have concluded the pursuit is not worth it as well. A Los Angeles official observed, "We made no effort to stop the Rams. We didn't try to go to the process of eminent domain. We did not try to generate a ground swell of protest. . . . We believed that Carroll Rosenbloom, like any other businessman in this country under our capitalist, free-enterprise system, had a right to move if he so desired." Harris, *The League*, p. 341.

40. See "Kelly Speech," Introduction, note 1. In exchange for these provisions, she offered tax waivers that would escalate annually, beginning at $3.5 million in the initial year. She also offered $1.7 million in sales tax credits and a "guaranteed stadium rental payment of $4.3 million." Ibid.

41. For example, the Mariners replaced the Pilots in Seattle following their departure, and the Royals replaced the A's following their departure from Kansas City.

42. It is certainly easier to find other events to fill a 16,000-seat arena on a regular basis than an 80,000-seat stadium. There are many concerts, circuses, ice shows, and other events available that will fill an arena, but only a very few concerts or special events that can fill an 80,000-seat stadium the way a football or baseball franchise can.

43. See Committee on the Judiciary, House of Representatives, "Antitrust Policy and Professional Sports," testimony of Ted Turner, p. 97.

44. See "For St. Pete's Sake," *Sports Illustrated*, Nov. 23, 1992, p. 14.

45. The *Sports Illustrated* article cited above compared the strategy of building a stadium to attract a franchise with the movie *Mondo Cane*, in which New Guinea Aborigines cleared a landing strip in the belief that it would attract one of the aircraft that passed overhead.

46. See Klobuchar, "Time Out: Millionaires of Sport Come Knocking Again," *Minneapolis Star Tribune*, April 29, 1992, B-3.

47. See "Shils Study," p. 51.

48. Ibid.

49. "Owners May Ask Aid for Target Center Debt," *Minneapolis Star Tribune*, March 1, 1992, B-2.

50. Gottlieb, "Trump Cleared to Build Domed Sports Stadium," *New York Times*, Dec. 5, 1985, B-3, col. 5. Part of Trump's enthusiasm may have been his desire to relocate his then-dormant USFL franchise to the stadium. In yet another example, the New England Patriots Stadium in Foxboro, Massachusetts, was financed with a Real Estate Investment Trust (REIT) in 1970. See Harris, *The League*, p. 125.

51. Trump even envisioned that this stadium could be the centerpiece for the Olympics in the year 2000. See Gottlieb, "Trump Cleared to Build Domed Sports Stadium."

52. As the deal was unraveling and the city requested proposals from other developers, Trump told the *New York Times*, "There's not a stadium in the United States that makes money. I offered—past tense—to build a stadium, and if the process is going to be long and difficult, I'm absolutely not interested." Ibid.

53. Reich, "Renovation of Coliseum Put in Limbo," *Los Angeles Times*, Dec. 31, 1991, A-1, col. 2. Revisions in the tax laws have also added to the difficulty in selling premium seats. Ibid.

54. See Reich, "Firm Gives Up on Renovating L.A. Coliseum," *Los Angeles Times*, Aug. 26, 1992, A-1, col. 4. (Similarly, the Rose Bowl in Pasadena had little success in selling luxury boxes at a "substantially lower" price [ibid].)

55. "Larger Small Cities; Salvation Through Sport," *The Economist* (U.K. Edition), June 10, 1989, p. 49.

56. See Baade and Dye, "The Impact of Stadiums and Professional Sports on Metropolitan Area Development," *Growth and Change* (Spring 1990): 5.

57. Spayd and Baker, "Elsewhere, Jury Out on New Stadium Benefits: Neighbors' Gripes, Development Problems Reflect Hardships Potomac Yard May Face," *Washington Post*, Aug. 2, 1992, B-1. But see Wells, "Property Values May

Jump Around Stadium," *Denver Business Journal,* Sept. 3, 1990, p. 1. The article states that the value of land in Toronto, Minneapolis, and St. Petersburg all increased after the construction of stadiums.

58. Ibid.

59. See (Spayd and Baker). H. Edwards, *The Sociology of Sport* (Homewood, Ill.: The Dorsey Press, 1973), citing J. Tunis, *$PORT$* (New York: The John Day Company, 1928), p. 24, and also in *Harpers,* "The Great God Football," 157 (November 1928): 742–52.

Index